THE
MAKING OF AMERICA
SERIES

CHESAPEAKE
VIRGINIA

D1597411

The U.S. frigate Constellation *was launched in 1797. Its construction was completed under the supervision of John L. Porter of the Gosport Navy Yard, near present-day Chesapeake. Porter later designed and built the Confederate ironclad* Merrimac.

ON THE COVER: *This photograph, which shows the interior of Hassell's Confectionery on Bainbridge Boulevard, was taken on December 6, 1939. Behind the counter are Jack Hassell (left) and his father, Bruce, serving an unidentified customer. A small rectangular sign on the wall advertises Capudine for headaches; a small amount of this substance was often mixed with Coca-Cola.*

THE
MAKING OF AMERICA
SERIES

CHESAPEAKE
VIRGINIA

RAYMOND L. HARPER

ARCADIA

Published by Arcadia Publishing,
an imprint of Tempus Publishing, Inc.
2 Cumberland Street
Charleston, SC 29401

Printed in Great Britain.

Library of Congress Catalog Card Number: 2001092153

For all general information contact Arcadia Publishing at:
Telephone 843-853-2070
Fax 843-853-0044
E-Mail sales@arcadiapublishing.com

For customer service and orders:
Toll-Free 1-888-313-2665

Visit us on the Internet at http://www.arcadiapublishing.com

The barque Belstone *was built at Charles J. Colonna's shipyard on the Eastern branch of the Elizabeth River in 1872. This painting, which was taken from a c. 1902 photograph, shows the vessel on the number 3 railway.*

Contents

ACKNOWLEDGMENTS

I would like to express my sincere appreciation to the many individuals and institutions who contributed their services, knowledge, and photographs used in *Chesapeake, Virginia*.

I am especially grateful to Richard W. Arnold; E.C. Beacham; Irwin M. Berent; Waverly L. Berkley III; Richard J. Cole, Office of the City Clerk, City of Chesapeake; W.W. Colonna Jr., chairman, Colonna's Shipyard, Inc.; Deputy John Downs, Chesapeake Sheriff Department; Terry Evans, director, Chesapeake Museum; Michelle Williams Grant, marketing department, Chesapeake General Hospital; Lil Hart, clerk of the Circuit Court of the City of Chesapeake; Casey Holtzinger, artist; Wayne Irby; Virginia Johnson; Dr. Raymond Jones, vice president, public radio services, WHRO; Captain Joel M. Kirshon, Chesapeake Sheriff Department; Mildred Miles; Dr. Bernard Miller; John R. Newhart, sheriff, City of Chesapeake; David Norton; Shirley Paxson; M.L. Phelps; Bill Pierce, former member of Chesapeake City Council; John Rudis, Chesapeake Fire Department; Teresa Rudis, St. Matthews Church; Stuart Smith, retired sergeant, Chesapeake Police Department; Patrick Wilkerson, photographer, Chesapeake Police Department; Jerome Yavner and Nina Wood, Waldenbooks, Greenbrier Mall.

I dedicate this book to my wife of 53 years, Emma Rock Harper; to our two daughters, Shari and Karen; our son-in-law, John Rudis; and our three grandchildren, Alexa Raye, Colby John, and Collin Steven Rudis.

INTRODUCTION

As cities go, Chesapeake is one of the newest in the State of Virginia. Having been formed by the merger of the City of South Norfolk and Norfolk County on January 1, 1963, it is now in its 39th year. Although the city is young in name, the roots from which it sprouted date back well before the 1600s. It was in this area and those nearby that the expedition that led to the first permanent English settlement of Tidewater Virginia took place.

In November 1775, the British invaded southeastern Virginia, and on December 9, 1775, Lord Dunmore's troops clashed with the American forces at Great Bridge, just a few yards from where the Civic Center now stands. After receiving a sound defeat in a battle that lasted less than half an hour, the British retired to the safety of their ships in the harbor at Norfolk.

After taking some time to think about the outcome of this battle, and having been refused provisions for his troops by the people of Norfolk, a very angry Dunmore decided to destroy Norfolk. About 4 p.m. on New Year's Day, 1776, his boats opened fire on the town and British sailors set fire to the wharves. One of the cannonballs was lodged into the wall of old St. Paul's Church and remains there to this day.

In 1793, work was begun on the Dismal Swamp Canal. Colonel William Byrd II first proposed the canal when he was in the area in the early eighteenth century, and the proposal was again made by George Washington in 1763. The canal opened in 1805. In 1801, the Gosport Navy Yard, which later was renamed the Norfolk Navy Yard, was acquired by the United States government from the Commonwealth of Virginia. The opening of the canal and the government acquisition of the naval yard both provided additional revenue to an already prosperous area.

The first local encounter of the Civil War was at Sewell's Point in Norfolk in May 1861. Other events of great significance in the area were the burning of the Gosport Navy Yard and the battle between the CSS *Virginia* (*Merrimac*) and the USS *Monitor*. When the war ended, Norfolk County took advantage of its natural resources. Its location near the coast, miles of riverfronts, deep harbors, and fertile farmland allowed residents to recover from the war and move into the new century.

The City of Chesapeake is composed of numerous small areas. Many of the older residents still refer to the names of the former communities, such as South

Norfolk, Portlock, Buell, Great Bridge, Pleasant Grove, Oak Grove, Fentress, Hickory, St. Brides, Deep Creek, Western Branch, Indian River, and possibly a few others that have slipped into the past.

In 1963, the former school systems of the City of South Norfolk and Norfolk County combined and became the Chesapeake Public School System. Since then, many new schools have been added to the system and others have been enlarged.

With the birth of Chesapeake, a new city seal was needed. The seal of the City of Chesapeake was designed by the late Kenneth Harris, a local artist who lived in the City of Norfolk. The original drawing of the seal is located at Chesapeake's Museum and Information Center on Bainbridge Boulevard.

By this time, I am sure the reader of this book is wondering why there is an in-depth chapter on Berkley. You are probably questioning my sanity and want to know what Berkley has got to do with the City of Chesapeake. Please allow me to explain. Originally the village of Berkley, which became a town on March 3, 1890, was a part of Norfolk County until it was annexed by the City of Norfolk on January 1, 1906. In the early 1880s, the founding fathers of Berkley had become wealthy from the many industries and business establishments in the town. Having done this, they began to acquire land farther to the south and on this land they built large handsome homes—most of them are still standing. It was like moving from a bustling town to the country. This new rural area to the south was eventually given the name South Norfolk. South Norfolk began as a village and then progressed to a town, then a city of the second class, and finally a city of the first class. Upon merger with Norfolk County, the area became a major part of the City of Chesapeake.

In 1930, E.H. Cuthrell established Cuthrell's Machine Works in what would later become Chesapeake. Probably the most noted articles manufactured at the works were practice space capsules like this one made for astronaut training during the National Aeronautics and Space Administration's Mercury and Gemini programs. A total of 30 capsules were built.

1. The Great Chesapeake

Although Sir Walter Raleigh had failed to establish a colony in Virginia and the idea had been abandoned, the late sixteenth century was a time in England when advances were being made in other fields. About ten years after Raleigh, others became eager to try again. Large trading companies already existed in other countries and in 1660, Queen Elizabeth chartered the East Indian Company. The organization of this company became the basis for the formation of the London Company of Virginia.

On April 10, 1606, King James I approved the division of this large company into two smaller companies. One became known as the London Company and the other was called the Plymouth Company. It was agreed that the London Company would settle in what became southern Virginia, which received its name from Queen Elizabeth, the "Virgin Queen," and that the Plymouth Company would settle in the northern part. Some land would also be open to both companies.

Under the charter of 1606, three small ships, the *Susan Constant*, *Godspeed*, and *Discovery,* were equipped and 104 colonists were sent to Virginia. A council of seven had been selected to rule the colony, one of the seven was to be president. It would not become known who the members of the council were until the colonists arrived in Virginia, however.

The expedition under the command of Captain Christopher Newport sailed from Blackwall in London on December 19, 1606. After a rough voyage, the land of Virginia was sighted about four in the morning on April 26, 1607. At daylight they passed between two capes that were eventually named Charles and Henry in honor of the sons of King James I and entered the Bay of Chesupioc (Chesapeake).

The colonists landed at Cape Henry on April 26 and planted a cross, taking possession of the land in the name of the king. They found fair meadows, "goodly tall" trees, and fresh water running through the woods. They named the point that gave their ships protection Point Comfort. After several days and several landings the ships proceeded up a broad river called the Powhatan, or King River. This they named the James River, after their king. The site that was selected for the first settlement became known as Jamestown.

On May 14, 1607, the men landed and set to work fortifying the area. At that time they learned that Captain Edward Maria Wingfield was president of the council, the other members of which included Captains George Kendall, John Ratcliffe, John Martin, Bartholomew Gosnold, Christopher Newport, and John Smith. Smith had been charged with mutiny and could not serve until he was acquitted, which he soon was.

Shortly after landing at Jamestown Captain Newport took 21 others up the river in search of a shortcut to the Pacific, little realizing how far away it was. But he did find a falls, and above them a Native American town "of twelve houses pleasantly seated on a hill." This was the site of present-day Richmond.

The first letter sent back to England from the new world reported the following observations:

> We are set down eighty miles within a River for breadth, sweetness of water, length navigable up into the country, deep and bold channell so stored with sturgeon and other sweet fish, as no man's fortune hath ever possessed the like. . . . The soil is most fruitfull, laden with oake, Ashe, Walnut trees, Poplar, Pine, sweet woods, Cedar, and others yet without names that yield gums pleasant as Frankincense and experienced amongst us for great vertue in healing green wounds and aches.

This copy of an early oil painting of Pocahontas was based on an engraving published in London before her death in 1617. Although there are many versions of her story, it is known that Pocahontas was instrumental in establishing friendly relations between her father, the chief Powhatan, and the English colonists at Jamestown. After converting to Christianity, marrying a colonist, and visiting England, the Native American princess died there of smallpox at the age of 22. She was buried in Gravesend, England.

This postcard from the 1907 Jamestown Exposition illustrates a popular version of the Pocahontas story: the young princess pleading with her father to spare John Smith's life.

Crude houses were built and after the construction of log huts was begun Christopher Newport returned to England. After his departure, John Smith made himself leader of the colonists.

Late in the fall of 1607 Smith explored the Chickahominy, was captured by Native Americans, carried before Opecancanough, and then Powhatan. It was then that Smith met the chief's daughter Pocahontas, "a maid of ten." There are several stories of how she persuaded her father to release Smith. It was not until many years after Pocahontas's death that Smith told his version of how she saved his life. In its final form, his story relates that the Indians placed Smith's head on two stones and were about to crush it with a war club when Pocahontas threw herself upon him and insisted that his life be spared. However it happened, Smith was finally released and he returned to Jamestown where he found that many of the settlers had died and the others were starving. As luck would have it Christopher Newport arrived soon after with supplies and they were saved.

In 1608 Smith set out again to explore the Chesapeake Bay and surrounding areas and drew a map that proved to be very accurate. Due to different languages and dialects the word Chesapeake was spelled and pronounced in many different ways. There is unfortunately no record of the name the Native Americans used for the bay, but there were several bestowed by early explorers. The first was Bahia de Santa Maria, then Bahia del Xacan. Another early name was Madre Agus, or Mother of Waters. The bay's present name was taken from the Chesapeake Indians who inhabited the shores of the Elizabeth River, the first inlet inside the capes. The name had many different spellings, including Chesapeach, Chesupioca, and Chissapiacke.

During the summer of 1608 the colonists were once again feeling the pangs of hunger, but Christopher Newport again arrived with more supplies and the colony was saved. This time he also brought additional settlers, one of whom was Anne Burras, who would later wed John Laydon in the colony's first marriage.

In the spring of 1609 some 500 new settlers arrived. About 120 of them settled in what became Richmond. Problems soon arose between the settlers and the Native Americans and John Smith went on a trip to try to settle the differences. On his return a bag of gunpowder exploded in his boat, severely injuring him and forcing him to return permanently to England.

Meanwhile Pocahontas was converted to Christianity and married the colonist John Rolfe, whose first wife had died in a wreck on the Bermuda islands. The marriage took place in the church at Jamestown and the couple honeymooned at Rolfe's estate Varina on the James River. As Rolfe's wife "Rebecka," Pocahontas visited England in 1616 and was received at the court of King James. In 1617 while making preparations to return home she became ill and died at the age of 22, leaving behind her husband and young son. Many Virginians claim to be descended from the son of John Rolfe and Pocahontas. It is possible that some of them are.

Four 100-year-old documents indicate that there were Native American settlements in the Great Neck area of Virginia Beach around the time of early

This drawing illustrates how a Chesapeake-area Native American farm may have appeared before the settlement of Jamestown. A tobacco crop can be seen growing at the top center and at the lower left between the second and third buildings.

The Powhatan Oak is known to have been growing at the time the colonists landed at Jamestown in 1607. At the 1907 Jamestown Exposition, when this photograph was taken, it was declared by forestry experts to be 350 years old.

Jamestown settlement. Residential development has destroyed much of that site; however, excavations have uncovered early burials and artifacts.

Early accounts of the Jamestown settlement made reference to the Chesapeake Indians. William Strachey wrote in his 1612 *History of Travell into Virginia Britania* that Chief Powhatan had exterminated the Chesapeake Indians. John Smith's map placed the village of the Chesapeakes in the vicinity of the Elizabeth River.

The colonists' first encounter with the Nansemond tribe was when Smith's barge was blown into the Nansemond River. According to his records the Indians were friendly at first but then attacked Smith and his crew, who retreated and burned the Indians' fields. He later talked them into surrendering and giving him many bushels of corn. Smith, it seems, was always getting into some kind of predicament but only he knew for sure how much of his stories were true.

When Jamestown was settled in 1607, the Nansemond village was located in the general vicinity of Reed's Ferry near Chuckatuck in what is now the city of Suffolk. The tribal king lived near Dumpling Island on the Nansemond River about 8 miles west of the Western Branch of the Elizabeth River. The population was about 1,200, with 300 bowmen. When the colonists were suffering from a severe shortage of food in 1608, some of the established settlers attempted to start a new colony in the Nansemond territory southeast of Jamestown. This ended in hostilities with the tribe.

Today the Nansemond is the only state-recognized tribe in Chesapeake. It is one of the few remaining tribes of the Powhatan Confederacy and it meets at the Indian United Methodist Church, which was founded in 1850.

In 1619, 90 young Englishwomen of unexceptionable character arrived in Jamestown. Prospective husbands arranged to pay the cost of the volunteers' outfits and passages with about $80 worth of tobacco. The governor issued a proclamation that maidens who betrothed themselves to more than one lover would be severely punished.

On November 18, 1618, the Virginia Company's London Council ordered that the Virginia Colony be divided into four large corporations. For purposes of local administration, each was to be a parish of the Church of England. Each was to have its own chief executive and military officer and later, either justices or a court of law. Since each corporation was an ecclesiastical parish, it was required to have a minister, churchwarden, and vestry. The Church of England was the only recognized church of the Colony of Virginia and Governor George Yeardley's instructions as of 1621 required him "to keep up religion of the Church of England as near as may be."

The next division of Virginia came in 1632–1634, when the colony was split into eight shires or counties. The original shires were Accamack (or Accomack), Charles City, Charles River (later York County), Elizabeth City, Henrico, James City, Warrosquyoake (later Isle of Wight), and Warwick River. The area from which Berkley and Chesapeake emerged was successively part of Elizabeth City County in 1634, New Norfolk County in 1636, Lower Norfolk County in 1637, and Norfolk County in 1691.

As the English moved into the lands around Chesapeake Bay, the Native Americans in the region resented seeing their land occupied by the white men. Powhatan was hostile to the English, but proved no match for John Smith and was finally forced to yield to most of the Englishman's demands. The chief saw his daughter Pocahontas captured, converted to Christianity, and finally married to one of the English. After his death, when Opecancanough became ruler, the uneasy peace was broken in an unexpected uprising during the spring of 1622. This was a severe blow to the colony, but in about eight months it recovered and became stronger than before.

2. THE AMERICAN REVOLUTION

Many events led up to the American Revolution. New taxes were imposed on the colonies and the spirit of resistance grew intense. In 1775 John Murray, Fourth Earl of Dunmore, the royal governor, broke off communications with the Virginia Assembly. On April 20, he removed the gunpowder from the public magazine in Williamsburg, the state capital at the time. The governor feared for his safety and took refuge with the British fleet in the York River. By July 1775, these ships had moved to the Elizabeth River near Norfolk, where they were soon strengthened by the arrival of additional warships. This location was where Dunmore planned to make his headquarters.

With the fleet anchored offshore, he was certain that he could reconquer the colony. On September 30, 1775, Dunmore sent his troops to Norfolk to destroy the printing press of John Holt and with it, the freedom of speech that had belonged to the people. Lord Dunmore and Virginia were now at the point of warfare. The "minutemen" of the upper counties were concentrating at Williamsburg, where they were making plans for a march on Norfolk. The Revolutionaries of Norfolk and Princess Anne, under the leadership of Colonel Matthew Phripp of the Norfolk militia, Colonel Arthur Lawson, and others, assembled and posted themselves at Kemp's Landing and other strategic points. Most of the Patriots in Norfolk had already left to join the militia, and there was an exodus along Church Street and the road leading to Great Bridge. On November 7, Dunmore issued a proclamation declaring martial law.

With a reinforcement of 60 men from St. Augustine, Florida, Dunmore was able to muster 200 soldiers and a few Tories for a descent on Great Bridge. The town of Great Bridge was approximately 10 miles from Norfolk Town along the Post Road and at the head of the canal on the Southern Branch of the Elizabeth River. This community was established on January 29, 1729, and its trustees included Samuel Willis, John Caldwell, Williams Grimes Sr., John Jones, John Hodges Jr., and Edward Hall Sr. Some years later, the town retrograded to a village.

The community received its name from a 40-yard-long bridge that crossed a marshy area on the Southern Branch of the Elizabeth River in the 1700s. There was marshy land on each side of the bridge, but there was an island of solid ground at both ends, and these islands were connected to the mainland by

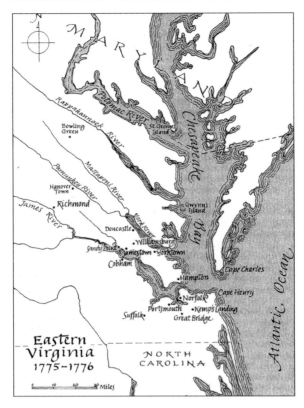

This map shows the area of Eastern Virginia around the mouth of the Chesapeake Bay during the years 1775–1776. It was during this period that Lord Dunmore led about 3,000 military, naval, and civilian forces from Williamsburg to Yorktown, Norfolk, Portsmouth, Kemp's Landing, Great Bridge, Gwynn's Island, and eventually up into Maryland.

causeways. It was the only crossing over the Southern Branch on the route from North Carolina to Norfolk. Great Bridge, at that time, was at the intersection of two roads from North Carolina and was a transfer point for tobacco, lumber, grain, pitch, tar, and turpentine. Because of its location, it was chosen as the site for one of the largest tobacco warehouses in the state.

Finding no militia at Great Bridge and learning that Colonel Lawson was at Kemp's Landing, Dunmore marched there and won an easy victory. Several men were killed, 2 drowned in their flight, and 14 were taken prisoner. On November 16, Dunmore marched into Norfolk. He found Scotch merchants and their clerks there and he forced their allegiance to the crown of England. He then made plans for fortification of the town and began construction of earthworks. This was one of many mistakes that he would make, for Norfolk's real strength against attack by land lay in the routes leading to the area.

Dunmore learned all too soon of his mistake in fortifying Norfolk. If the British had erected works at Bachelor's Mill on the edge of the Dismal Swamp and at Great Bridge, the Virginians would probably never have gotten near the village of Great Bridge. This was a place of natural strength, for the Southern Branch of the Elizabeth River flowed between marshes extending approximately 150 yards on either side. From the northern side, a long causeway crossed the marsh to an island of firm earth, where a wooden bridge 40 yards in length had been erected over the stream to a similar island on the other bank. This island in turn was connected with the village of Great Bridge by another causeway over the marsh on the southern side. On the south island were a number of warehouses, where goods were taken on and off the riverboats. The British put up a stockade fort on the north island and planted guns there.

During all this, the Virginians under the command of Colonel William Woodford, along with Lieutenant Colonel Scott and Major Thomas Marshall, had left Williamsburg, crossed the James River, and headed for Suffolk where there were large amounts of stores and provisions. Major Marshall, who was later promoted to colonel, was the father of John Marshall. In 1775 John Marshall was a 20-year-old militiaman and the following year he joined the Continental Army. One of President John Adams's last acts in office was the appointment of John Marshall as chief justice of the U.S. Supreme Court.

When Woodford's forces reached Great Bridge, they threw up breastworks across the southern end of the causeway, which they manned with a few men. The main force was posted in the village behind it. There, they remained for several days, awaiting reinforcements from North Carolina under Colonel Robert Howe. Woodford could not have forced his way over the Southern Branch, and to charge across the causeway and bridge against the British would have been costly. To flank the position on the right was not possible because of the swamp, and on the left, the British sloops guarded the river. Eventually, the enemy took the initiative. A slave of Major Marshall's faked desertion to the British and informed Dunmore that the Virginians numbered no more than 300. Remembering how the militia had fled at Kemp's Landing, and thinking these men to be of the same caliber, Dunmore decided to attack.

The royal governor assembled all his available regulars, 60 Tories, and some sailors from the warships, and this force, along with 30 whites and 90 slaves

This image of the Battle of Great Bridge shows the action as it is believed to have looked on December 9, 1775.

already there, brought the total up to several hundred men. On the morning of December 9, 1775, the Virginians heard reveille in the British fort, which was followed by the blast of cannons and muskets. The British regulars appeared first and were followed by the Tories and slaves. The foremost ranks carried planks, which were used to cover the broken part of the bridge. This permitted the troops and two cannons to cross to the south island. After burning a few houses and piles of shingles, they opened fire on the American breastwork. The British regulars, under the command of Captain Charles Fordyce, then advanced over the south causeway. The Americans, behind their breastworks, waited. Lieutenant Edward Travis ordered them to hold their fire until the enemy was within 50 yards. Then, when given the signal, they opened fire. Some of the forward troops were killed, others were wounded, and the back ranks began to falter. Captain Fordyce waved them on, but as he approached the breastworks, he fell mortally wounded. It was reported that he had 14 wounds in his body.

British Captain Samuel Leslie tried to rally the troops. The Tories and those in the rear had not advanced beyond the island and two cannons continued to play upon the Virginians. At this point in the battle, Colonel Woodford brought up reinforcements, opened heavy fire, and forced the British in retreat across the

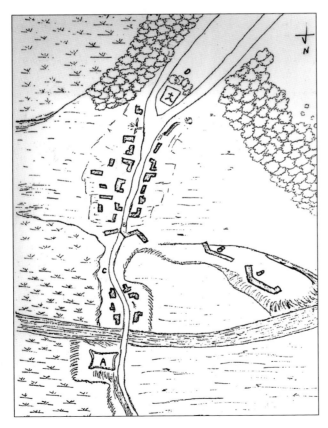

In this map of Great Bridge from the time of the battle, A is the fort built by Lord Dunmore's troops, B indicates the fortifications built by the Americans, and C is the causeway across the swamp. The great bridge itself is directly in front of the British fort, crossing the Southern Branch of the Elizabeth River.

Facing Battlefield Boulevard, the Island Wharf shopping area stands today where more than 200 years ago the Battle of Great Bridge took place during the Revolutionary War.

bridge. As the firing ceased, some of the Virginians climbed over the breastworks to assist the British wounded. Captain Leslie reportedly stepped out in front of the fort and bowed his thanks for the consideration shown by the American troops. On the evening of the battle, the British retreated.

With all that took place that day, it was reported that the British lost at least 40 men, and the single injury in the American ranks was a slight wound in the hand of one soldier. The actual battle lasted no more than 30 minutes.

Fearing that he could not hold Norfolk, Dunmore retired to his gunboats in the harbor. Afterwards, he sent ashore under flag of truce for provisions, and when they were refused him, he went into a rage and was determined to destroy the town. He sent a warning that the women and children should be taken out of harm's way. About 4 p.m. on New Year's Day, 1776, the boats started up a heavy cannonade and parties of sailors under this protection managed to set fire to the wharves and practically burn the entire town. Old St. Paul's Church on Church Street (now St. Paul Boulevard) was about the only building of importance that escaped the flames. A cannonball, however, was lodged in one of the walls of the church and remains there to this day.

Between July and October 1777, an oath of allegiance was passed among the colonists:

> I do swear or affirm that I renounce and refuse all allegiance to George the third, King of Great Britain, his heirs and successors and that I will

be faithful and bear true allegiance to the Commonwealth of Virginia as a free and independent State, and that I will not, at anytime do or cause to be done any matter or thing that will be prejudicial or injurious to the freedom and independence there of as declared by congress and also that I will discover and make known to some one Justice of the Peace for the said State all treasons or traitorous conspiracies which I now or hereafter shall know to be formed against this or any of the United States of America.

This petition was first dated and signed by Cornilous Calvert and John Wilson on July 18, 1777. The final page stated, "To the oath or affirmation of allegiance to this Commonwealth before me given under my hand and seal this 17th Day of October 1777." Matthew Godfrey also signed it, and he then listed the names of three persons who refused to sign the oath.

For the immediate vicinity, there was nothing more of special moment until 1779, when the English, under General Edward Matthews, landed in Portsmouth and made it his headquarters. The British captured a large number of vessels, which were at that time on the Gosport anchorage, and forced the garrison to leave Fort Nelson, which was built on the present site of the Naval Hospital. A few months later, General Alexander Leslie added 3,000 troops to Matthews's forces, and together they ruined a large amount of property across Tidewater Virginia. The next year, the notorious American traitor Benedict Arnold held the town with orders to do as much damage as possible, to spare nobody, and to leave nothing.

Late in the war the British, in great numbers, returned to Virginia and Great Bridge was again fortified. A leading Loyalist unit known as "the Queen's Rangers," under command of John Graves Simcoe, was stationed at a newly established location; however, the British had apparently learned an important lesson in 1775 and there was not another battle at Great Bridge. After having served the crown as one of its brightest commanding officers, Simcoe was appointed the first lieutenant governor of Upper Canada. The Revolutionary War continued until Lord Cornwallis went to his final and conclusive defeat at Yorktown in 1781. The Queen's Rangers inflicted no damage because they were poorly equipped, many even without shoes.

Cornwallis was hemmed in at Yorktown and forced to surrender in October 1781. Although the war had ended, peace terms were not concluded between England and its former colonies for two more years. The devastation in Norfolk, Portsmouth, and vicinity was more complete than in most other areas. Some parts were described as nothing more than piles of trash and heaps of pure rubbish; however, by 1779 reconstruction had begun to take place and things were looking up. Norfolk County had experienced some damage to buildings and fields. The farmers began gradually clearing the land and the crops came back larger than before. Today those fields are an integral part of the City of Chesapeake.

3. THE WAR BETWEEN THE STATES

In the year 1861 the City of Portsmouth, which was the seat of Norfolk County, had a population of about 9,000 persons. The population of Norfolk County was approximately 12,000. The Gosport Navy Yard, the largest of its kind in the United States, was located at the southern end of the city and usually employed 1,200 to 1,500 workers. The city, for the most part, was prosperous and contented.

When the question of seceding from the Union came before the people on February 4, 1861, in the form of an election for delegates to the State Convention, the two representatives running on the Union ticket won by a large majority over those who ran on the Secession ticket. Union sentiment was predominant in the State Convention. Also in February, a secessionist congress had convened in Montgomery, Alabama, and declared a provisional government, voting Jefferson Davis president of the Confederate States of America.

Several Southern states had already seceded from the Union by this time, and instead of trying to persuade them to return, the men who controlled the new Republican-influenced administration were in favor of forcing them back into the Union. President Abraham Lincoln, who had taken office on March 4, 1861, later issued a call for 75,000 troops and assigned Virginia its share in response to the violent takeover of Fort Sumter in South Carolina. It became evident that Virginia could not remain neutral but would have to fight with or against the other Southern states. The State Convention passed the ordinance of secession on April 17, 1861, and the resolution was to be submitted to the people for vote on the fourth Thursday of May, but for all intents and purposes, the state was out of the Union after the convention.

In the spring of 1861, the U.S. Army was a small organization of 16,000 regulars, most of whom were scattered along the Western frontier. Of this number there were approximately 1,100 officers and more than 300 of them had resigned their commissions and sided with the South.

The U.S. Navy was in the same shape. About half the fleet, including its most powerful steam frigates, were out of commission, obsolete, and unfit for service. Personnel consisted of 1,457 line and staff officers, 7,600 enlisted men, and about 1,400 marines. Some 250 officers submitted their resignations to join the Confederacy. Secretary of the Navy Gideon Welles chose not to accept them, but instead decided to dismiss these men from the naval service.

Many of the ships that saw action in the Civil War were built at the Gosport Navy Yard. This c. 1861–1865 view shows several of them near a wharf lined with cannons either recently unloaded or waiting to be loaded.

The navy yards were full of corruption. Most civilian workers received their jobs on the basis of party affiliation and were assessed contributions by the district congressmen. Usually when a new president came into office, the workers were replaced by those who favored the new administration. President Lincoln chose not to do this. This proved to be an error in judgment because the nearly 1,000 civilian workers at the Gosport yard remained Democratic in politics and Southern in sympathy.

The Gosport Navy Yard, which was about three-quarters of a mile long, was actually located across the Elizabeth River from the City of Norfolk. In 1861, it was under the command of Commodore Charles S. McCauley, who was as antiquated as the ships. He had served the U.S. Navy for 52 of his 68 years. McCauley had entered the navy as a midshipman in 1809 and served on a frigate during the War of 1812. At his command were only 16 officers, less than 100 sailors, and 60 marines. Most of the officers were loyal to the South.

The yard was completely equipped for building the largest and most modern warships, and five steam vessels had already been launched from there. The yard's most valuable asset was its new granite masonry dry dock. One of only two in the nation, it could berth any vessel in the fleet at that time. Across the Elizabeth River from the yard were the powder magazine at Fort Norfolk and the gun carriage at St. Helena. Neither was guarded.

McCauley was uncertain as to what course of action to take, for he had received no instructions from the Navy Department. His last orders, which were received April 16, ordered him to outfit the *Merrimac* and to send her with the other vessels capable of being moved, together with the ordinance and stores, out of reach of potential danger. The commodore thought the order from the Navy Department was to abandon the Navy Yard and not to fire on the City of Portsmouth. In light of the last orders he had received from Washington, McCauley was determined to leave with what he could take and destroy the rest.

The continuous movement of trains on the Norfolk and Petersburg Railroad within hearing distance of the Navy Yard led McCauley to believe that there had been a large influx of troops into the area. The noise was instigated by General William Mahone, who was then president of the railroad, for the purpose of creating just such an impression.

Destruction of the yard began about noon on April 20, and the frigate *Merrimac* was the first object of those assigned to the destruction detail. The bilge cocks of the *Cumberland* were opened, and she filled with water and settled to the bottom.

This is a drawing of John L. Porter's model of the Merrimac. *Porter, who supervised the construction of several U.S. vessels, was stationed at Gosport in April 1861 and witnessed its destruction by Federal troops, after which he resigned his commission and offered his services to the governor of Virginia.*

This photograph of the USS Monitor *was taken shortly after the battle with the* Merrimac. *Several dents can be seen in its turret.*

After the 12 o'clock bell was rung for the workers to break for lunch, the gates of the Navy Yard were closed and no one was permitted to enter without the approval of the commodore. The work of destruction then proceeded very quickly. The *Germantown, Plymouth, Dolphin, Delaware,* and *Columbus* were scuttled. In late afternoon, the sloop-of-war *Pawnee,* under Captain Hiram Paulding, docked at the Navy Yard, and her crew were added to the wrecking force. Captain Paulding gave the order to torch the buildings. Several were filled with stores, which were also destroyed. One of the buildings contained large amounts of liquor, and the sailors filled themselves until they were too drunk to continue the work of destruction. Captain Paulding was later given the rank of commodore and was the Navy's senior line officer.

It was reported also that there was an attempt to blow up the large stone dry dock, and when the Portsmouth military companies marched into the Navy Yard the next day, they found loose powder all over the dry dock. The cause of the failure to ignite the powder remained a mystery until February of the next year.

The man in charge of the detail lit the fuse but instead of igniting the powder, threw the fuse overboard. The reason he gave for doing this was that he had a number of friends in Portsmouth and the amount of powder used would have blown some of the stone beyond the Navy Yard and would have possibly killed someone.

It did not take the Confederates long to get the Navy Yard back into operation. The salvage and repair was accomplished under the new commandant, Flag Officer French Forrest. The most noteworthy achievement of all was the conversion of the *Merrimac* into the ironclad CSS *Virginia*. On May 30, Forrest wrote Robert E. Lee, "We have the Merrimac up and just putting her in dry dock."

On March 8, 1862, this transformed frigate sank the *Cumberland* and captured the frigate *Congress*. The next day she met the *Monitor*, the Federal prototype ironclad vessel, and the historic battle of the ironclads took place. This was the most notable event of the war within the bounds of Norfolk County. The outcome of the battle seems to have depended largely on the point of view of the witness. While one claimed "the *Monitor* was the first to get enough and retired

Pictured here is Sergeant Carey Daniel Woodward of Company F, 15th Virginia Cavalry. Members of Company F belonged mostly to St. Brides Parish of Norfolk County. After the war, Woodward spent most of the rest of his life farming, but he also served as a constable in Norfolk County.

25

This young and unknown soldier of the Civil War appears ready for action, although when this photograph was taken he probably had no idea what was in store for him. He has attached his bayonet and carries an Army Colt in his waist belt.

behind the *Minnesota*," most historians contend that the battle was a draw as the *Monitor* had succeeded in protecting other Federal vessels. Later in the war the CSS *Virginia* was run ashore, dismantled, and burned by her crew to prevent capture by Federal forces occupying the area.

The people of Norfolk County suffered through four years of destruction. Farms were destroyed, livestock and crops were stolen, and most of the wooden schools were dismantled or burned. When the war ended, Virginia faced the monumental task of reconstruction. The state's industrial base had been destroyed, the railroads were in ruins, and the agrarian economy was devastated. Many thousands of Virginians were surviving only on the rations distributed by the Union army. Thousands of returning soldiers and others were without employment or a place to live. Also, more than 30,000 Virginians had died during the war.

On May 9, 1865, President Andrew Johnson recognized Francis H. Pierpont as provisional governor of Virginia. The government originally was based in Alexandria, but Pierpont soon moved his administration to Richmond, where he hoped to restore his state to its former status in the union.

In October 1865, a full state government was elected along with congressional representatives. The acceptance of the representatives would have rendered restoration complete, but Congress refused to seat them. The presidential plan of reconstruction was rejected and Congress undertook the work itself.

Early in December 1865, the legislature convened in Richmond, enacted vagrant and contract laws, wiped out of the statute books all laws relating to slavery, and placed African Americans on the same footing as whites, with the exceptions that they could not vote or hold office.

The congressional reconstruction acts were passed in March 1867 and the state became Military District Number One. The acts gave African Americans the vote. About one year after the close of the war the relationship between whites and blacks was reportedly cordial.

Prosperity returned to the Norfolk area when the railroads began bringing coal and produce from the west and points south. The rails were a boon to Norfolk and also to the farms and villages of Norfolk County. New industries grew up along the Eastern and Southern Branches of the Elizabeth River, and new businesses and housing appeared near the railroad line.

When the war started, the boys and young men of what is now Chesapeake had dreams of military glory. Little did they realize that it would be a long and bloody war with a very high number of casualties. One from the area who survived was William Henry Stewart, who early on met with a group of friends at Pleasant Grove Baptist Church and organized what became known as the Jackson Greys. Stewart was elected captain and William Wallace first lieutenant. Wallace eventually became captain of the Greys and Stewart finished the war as a lieutenant colonel in the Confederate Army.

4. Berkley

In 1728, when Colonel William Byrd II stopped on his way to oversee the surveying of the dividing line between North Carolina and Virginia, he referred to the area as Powder Point. This name came from the fact that the town of Norfolk kept a magazine there for the storage of gunpowder. Later, the name was changed to Ferry Point because the Norfolk County ferry docked at the end of what would become Chestnut Street. Still later in the eighteenth century, the name was again changed—this time to Washington Point. The name Washington originated in the tradition that George Washington visited the place with a view of locating the nation's capital there. It was further stated that the idea was abandoned because the point was too near the coast to be fortified.

Earlier, in 1691, Lower Norfolk County was divided into Norfolk and Princess Anne Counties. At that time, the legislature directed that a new courthouse be erected in "Norfolk Towne." Work on the courthouse was begun in the summer of 1691 and the structure was completed in 1694. This location was on the north side of Norfolk's Main Street. In 1789, the Virginia Legislature chose Powder Point as the location for the next Norfolk County courthouse. At that time, a suitable building was not available, so a lot was purchased from Edmund Allmand for 25 English pounds. Eventually, the courthouse was built at the corner of what later became Walnut and Pine Streets. According to court records, the first court session was held on December 1, 1789, at the home of a Mrs. Shafer in Powder Point. The county court was moved to Portsmouth in 1801, where it remained until the City of Chesapeake was formed in 1963. The former courthouse was afterwards used as a meeting place for church groups and the few lodge organizations of the day. The building later became a gristmill and after that, served as a knitting mill operated by George W. Simpson, his brother Sam, and W.L. Bailie. The property was bought by Sam Fox several years after this and converted into an apartment house.

On December 20, 1787, under the provisions of the General Assembly of Virginia, the first marine hospital in the United States was erected at the foot of Chestnut Street. It was established for the reception of aged and disabled seamen and was initially presided over by Mrs. Mary Logan Morton. On May 3, 1807, the east wing was destroyed by fire. The building served many other functions during its life, one being a barracks for Confederate troops during the War Between the

States. It was later taken over by the Federal government. By 1896, it housed the Berkley Military Institute (BMI). Professor J.W. Roberts served as its principal, and among its teachers were Professor S.M. Smith, Miss Jennie Swain, Miss Margaret Tatem, Miss Ella Boone, and Miss Mamie Whitley. BMI was actually a co-educational high school with a military department. Major Tarrell of Norfolk directed the military, and B.H. Gibson, who later became mayor of South Norfolk, was captain of the school soldiers. Early in the twentieth century, Paul Garrett of Garrett's Winery acquired the old hospital and had it totally remodeled. It then served as a residence for his family and became known as the Garrett Mansion. During World War I, this same building served as an entertainment center for enlisted men and was known as the Imperial Club. After standing for almost 150 years, the building was torn down in 1933. In years to come, local folks would remember this landmark as the old Garrett home.

On the eastern side of the Southern Branch of the Elizabeth River, west of St. Helena and south of what is now Berkley Avenue, was the residential section of Montalant. According to tradition, it was first inhabited by a French nobleman of that name, who came to the area about 1790 to escape the French Revolution. According to local legend, he built his home with a high fence surrounding it and lived there with several of his followers in complete seclusion until the war was over. St. Helena, Ivy, Montalant, and Water were the main streets running through Montalant.

In 1780, the Virginia General Assembly approved a tax for the construction of this, the first marine hospital in the United States, located in Washington, Norfolk County.

About 1846, St. Helena, the land situated south of Washington Point and directly across the Elizabeth River from the Gosport (later named Norfolk) Navy Yard, was sold to the U.S. government. The property was used as a naval training station and was utilized by the Gosport Navy Yard to relieve its overcrowded grounds. In later years, the U.S. Coast Guard used a part of it. After World War II, the abandoned barracks became college classrooms to accommodate returning veterans wanting to further their education. The location was a part of the Norfolk Division of the College of William and Mary-VPI; the students named it the "St. Helena Institute of Technology" and, using the first letter of each major word, gave it a not-so-appropriate acronym. The property was later deeded to the City of Norfolk, the old buildings were removed, and a modern elementary school was built on the site.

CONNECTION TO GENERAL DOUGLAS MACARTHUR

Berkley is one of the oldest communities in Virginia. Its history began when John Herbert received land grants along the Elizabeth River in 1664 and again in 1667. This land is at that point where the Southern Branch meets the Eastern Branch of the Elizabeth River. Practically this entire section was at one time owned by the Herbert family and was known as Herbertsville.

The Herberts were boatbuilders and ship captains, and in 1728, Henry Herbert, a descendant of John, established a shipyard that remained in operation until 1828. Henry died in 1778, leaving operation of the business to other members of the family. Some of the ships produced at the yard saw service during the Revolutionary War and also in the undeclared war with France that took place

Riveredge was the Herbert/Hardy house where General Douglas MacArthur's mother, Mary Pinckney Hardy, was born in 1852. The house was later the location of several businesses, but it was neglected and eventually deteriorated. What remained was purchased by the owners of Colonna's Shipyard in 1949 and demolished in 1951.

during the administration of President John Adams. Several generations of the Herbert family built two brick homes facing the Elizabeth River. The houses were so large that they must have appeared as two fortresses protecting the sea lanes. At this time, the area was mostly wooded and was not yet a town. It was very sparsely settled, and the land was divided into large plantations. The Herbert homes were on the waterfront near the spot where the Berkley Bridge would later be built in 1916. This area was also known as "Berkley Flats." The family burying ground was situated about 200 feet from the houses.

In the 1840s, Enoch Herbert, who then owned the property, decided to "Go West," like many adventurous Americans of the time, and he began to sell some of his property. His home and the section east of Main Street and north of Poplar Avenue were sold to Thomas Asbury Hardy in 1846. Herbert gave the property, which now includes Poplar Avenue to Liberty Street and that east of Main Street, to his daughter Lydia, who married Thomas Nash.

Local entrepreneur Thomas Hardy was born in Bertie County, North Carolina, in 1800. When he was 26, he moved to Norfolk, became successful as a cotton and fertilizer broker, and was the owner of a basket and barrel factory. In 1831, he married Elizabeth Margaret Pierce, a Norfolk native, and they lived in a brick house at the northeast corner of Granby and Market Streets. In later years, this corner became the location of Smith and Welton's department store. The home sold to Hardy was known as "Riveredge" and was said to contain at least 20 rooms and a brick tunnel leading from the house to the barn and an escape route down to the river's edge, where boats were anchored. The walls inside the tunnel had metal rings sunk into them. It has never been proven, but it has been assumed that the Hardys were involved in the slave trade and that these rings were used to anchor the slaves while they were waiting in the tunnel to be transported to market.

On March 22, 1852, Mary Pinckney "Pinky" Hardy was born at Riveredge to Thomas and Elizabeth Hardy; she was one of 14 children. When Federal forces captured Norfolk in 1862, the home was turned into a hospital, and Mary found refuge on one of her father's plantations in North Carolina. In 1872, while attending the Mardi Gras festival in New Orleans, she met a young army officer by the name of Arthur MacArthur. A native of Springfield, Massachusetts, MacArthur had joined the army at the age of 17 and fought with the Union forces during the conflict. On May 19, 1875, Mary Pinckney Hardy married Arthur MacArthur in a ceremony performed by Reverend Matthew O'Keefe at Riveredge. Two of Pinky's brothers were graduates of the Virginia Military Institute, and during the Civil War, they had served under General Robert E. Lee. They did not like the idea of their sister marrying a Yankee and refused to attend the wedding. The MacArthurs' first two sons, Arthur III and Malcome, were born at Riveredge. Malcome died of measles when he was five years old and was buried at Cedar Grove Cemetery in Norfolk.

Their third son, Douglas, was born on January 26, 1880, at Fort Dodge, which is now part of Little Rock, Arkansas. On Tuesday, June 13, 1899, the train stopped at West Point, long enough for Douglas and his mother to disembark. Pinky spent

31

the next four years living at Craney's Hotel, where she could keep an eye on her son as he attended school. From the hotel, she could see the lamp in his room and knew when he was studying. By this time, her other son, Arthur III, had graduated from the Naval Academy at Annapolis, Maryland, but it appears that Pinky had abandoned her husband. In 1903, Douglas graduated first in his class from West Point, went on to pursue a military career, served in both World Wars I and II, and during World War II, became the famous general of the American forces in the Pacific theater.

Mrs. MacArthur's father, Thomas Asbury Hardy, had died in 1876, and her mother died about five years later. It was after this that Riveredge was sold to the Ryland Institute, a school for young ladies. During the 1930s, the house consisted of three large sections. Signs painted on each section indicated the various commercial ramifications through which the fine old home had passed. One of the signs proclaimed, "Main Street Belt Line Terminals." The building remained vacant for many years and was the victim of vandals, fire, and the elements. In 1949, the 28-acre tract was purchased by Colonna's Shipyard for $50,000. Former U.S. Senator A. Willis Robertson proposed a bill to establish the home as a national monument. Soon after the bill was proposed, architects checked the building. Their decision was that the house had to be rebuilt on the inside. The roof was in ruins and the plaster had fallen in all 20 rooms. The architects estimated that it would take at least $100,000 to restore the old home. After this, there was a fire that completely destroyed the interior of the house and the only thing to do was to demolish the structure. It was torn down in 1951 and a part of the early history of Berkley was lost. Enough of the original bricks were salvaged to build a wall around a small park with plaques memorializing the Hardy family and General MacArthur's mother. In September 1951, the general, his wife, and son came to Norfolk to dedicate the park. The bronze plaque reads, "Birthplace of Mary Pinckney Hardy / The Mother of General Douglas MacArthur." She passed away on December 3, 1935, and is buried in Arlington.

General Douglas MacArthur died at Walter Reed Hospital on Sunday April 5, 1964, at the age of 84. His body lay in state in three different cities before the funeral service was conducted on Saturday at the old Saint Paul's Episcopal Church in Norfolk. After the service, the general's body was entombed in the former courthouse at the foot of City Hall Avenue in Norfolk, Virginia. His wife, Jean Faircloth MacArthur, lived to be more than 100 years old and was buried beside her husband. This structure is now known as MacArthur Memorial and houses a large collection of memorabilia regarding the famed general's life and achievements. In March 1999, a very large shopping mall was erected nearby and given the name MacArthur Mall.

BERKLEY TAKES SHAPE

Berkley's beginning as a progressive community began after the Civil War, when Lycurgus Berkley Sr. (1827–1881), a wealthy partner of the firm of Berkley, Miller and Company, wholesale dry goods merchants of Norfolk, began to develop it as a town. Berkley was born in 1827 on the family plantation, which was called "The Glen." The plantation was near the Fairfax, Virginia courthouse on the road to Warrenton and had been in the Berkley family for several generations. Lycurgus was the eldest of four children born to John Walker Berkley and his second wife, the widow Mary Perry Carpenter. John Walker Berkley died of natural causes while the battle of Second Manassas was being fought near his home.

Lycurgus Berkley came to Norfolk in 1847, when he was just 20 years of age. He married Eliza Ann Middleton of Ferry Point, Norfolk County. She was the only daughter of Captain John Sutton Middleton, a seafaring man whose family had settled on the shores of the Elizabeth River prior to 1765. Following his marriage to Eliza, they made their home in a rambling colonial homestead that occupied the land bounded by Chestnut, Middleton, Walnut, and Westmoreland Streets. This residence was demolished in 1904.

Eliza's family owned much of the land on which the town named for her husband was built. Berkley acquired considerable land of his own in the area and became a man of substantial wealth. He subdivided the farm adjoining the homestead, laid out the streets, gave them names, and took a leading

Lycurgus Berkley came to Norfolk in 1847 at the age of 20. He became wealthy and took a leading part in the development of the community, which would eventually be named for him. Berkley donated land for four churches and also gave them financial support. In 1852 he married Eliza Ann Middleton of Ferry Point.

part in development of the community. He even donated sites for four churches, giving financial support as well, and invited outside interest to invest in his development.

The following was written to describe Lycurgus Berkley, the man:

> His life was actuated by noble impulses. He was large-hearted, genial and courteous and had a host of friends. He was especially interested in young men and delighted to aid them both financially and by wise advice. He took but little interest in politics, beyond demanding an honest administration of local and state affairs. To each of the churches established in the new town he gave $500 in cash and a site upon which to build. He was a fine businessman, having the progressive spirit, a courtly gentleman, and he predicted a great future for his little town.

When Lycurgus Berkley died in 1881, the small community was rated as the most prosperous in the Tidewater region. The town of Berkley was created by an act of the General Assembly of Virginia, which was sponsored by John M. Berkley, a resident and a member of the House of Delegates from Norfolk County. The act was approved on March 3, 1890. John Berkley, a son of the founder, was elected the town's first mayor.

MAGNOLIA CEMETERY

In 1861, the men of the village of Washington joined the forces of Robert E. Lee to serve the Southern states. Three unknown soldiers were buried in a field that became Magnolia Cemetery. Later, many others, including local residents who were then soldiers, were laid to rest in the Confederate Square section of the cemetery. Magnolia is located at Lancaster Street near Berkley Avenue and is the site of more than 9,000 graves.

A few years after the War Between the States, an annual Memorial Day parade became a tradition in Berkley. In the early 1900s, Police Sergeant James F. Tatem led the assembled marchers. When on duty, the sergeant could usually be found behind his desk at the combined police and fire station on Liberty Street. On Memorial Day, he dressed in the uniform of a Confederate cavalry officer, with high-topped black leather boots and a gray felt hat with a long, fluffy feather attached. Tatem always led the procession on a spirited horse. The parade began on Chestnut Street, near the ferry dock, and moved up Berkley Avenue to Magnolia Cemetery, where there was a stand for the master of ceremonies and the speaker of the day. After most of the old Berkley families died or moved to the other side of the river, the parade was discontinued and Sergeant Tatem joined forces with the people of Portsmouth. Each Memorial Day, he led their parade to the Cedar Grove Cemetery. In May 1932, while leading the parade into Cedar Grove Cemetery, Sergeant Tatem died in the saddle. He was still wearing his Confederate uniform.

BERKLEY BUSINESS

The town's accessibility to the sea and the availability of raw materials brought many investors from outside the local area in the latter 1800s and early 1900s. Lumber mills, box factories, knitting mills, and shipyards began to spring up and fortunes were made overnight. A large number of outsiders made Berkley their home.

Along the waterfront in 1889 were the lumber mills of Le Kies & Collins, Baker Salvage Company, the ferry wharf at the end of Chestnut Street, Fray Bros. sawmill, Norfolk & Southern Railroad wharves, Thomas boatyard, E.M. Tilley Lumber Company at Montalant, Tunis & Serpell Lumber Company along the Southern Branch, and the Sandy Point mills of Greenleaf Johnson & Son. Colonna's Shipyard, the residence of C.J. Colonna, and property owned by B.A. Colonna were situated on the Eastern Branch of the Elizabeth River near the Norfolk & Western Railroad.

In 1875 Charles Jones Colonna, a 26-year-old ship carpenter, built a marine railway with a capacity of 40 tons. His railway was so limited that he could haul only small boats, and therefore his profit was very small. However, there were a few things in his favor. There were numerous sawmills located at nearby Washington Point with an unlimited supply of lumber of all sizes and kinds. There was also plenty of timber in the forests that covered much of the area. Water

Charles J. Colonna designed and built this small shipyard in 1875 near the confluence of the Eastern and Southern Branches. The family business has grown and is now more than 125 years old. This painting is based on information from shipyard archives and from the accounts of Colonna family members.

transportation was cheap and dependable and many places could not be reached by land travel. All manner of transport was by water; produce was brought from the farms of Norfolk County to the markets of Norfolk by way of boats. Most of the boats were of wooden construction, and their repairs required the skills of ship carpenters, riggers, sailmakers, wood caulkers, painters, and blacksmiths.

The marine railway and shipyard were located in the Berkley section of Norfolk County on the Eastern Branch of the Elizabeth River. Its location was on the east side of Main Street near the old Hardy home (formerly the Herbert plantation) and diagonally across the river from downtown Norfolk. A horse-drawn turnstile, which was a piece of marine railway hauling machinery, was used to draw the vessels out of the water.

Colonna persevered in his business endeavor, and in five years he found it necessary to enlarge his plant. The property that Colonna was using was leased, so in order to enlarge his operation, he had to purchase a place. In doing so, he was able to put in a plant with a capacity of 500 tons. His prosperity steadily increased, and six years later, he constructed a railway with a capacity of 2,000 tons. In 1899, Colonna bought the John L. Thomas plant. Three years later, he purchased the shipyard adjoining his own, which was the property of W.A. Graves. Interestingly, Colonna had at one time been employed by Graves.

Logs, which were used for the manufacture of lumber, came mostly from the forests and swamps of North Carolina and the neighboring counties of Virginia. A large number of logs were harvested from the Great Dismal Swamp, and they were floated through canals that connected to the Elizabeth River. Distribution of the lumber was mostly by sea along the Atlantic coast, with rare shipments to the interior by rail. Lumber was also exported to Hamburg, London, and Liverpool markets.

Among the manufacturers that assisted Berkley in making rapid strides in the textile industry was the underwear factory of the Berkley Knitting Mills. G.W. Simpson served as the mill's president, and William L. Bailie Jr. was the manager. The establishment of the Chesapeake and Elizabeth Knitting Mills brought a large number of people to the area in the late 1880s. Foster Black operated both mills and after his death in 1903, William Sloane acquired them. Another manufacturer of importance to the area, the Cottonseed Oil and Fiber Company of Philadelphia

One of Berkley's early waterfront businesses, the Tunis & Serpell Lumber Company employed 500 men in its mill and logging camps on the Eastern Branch starting in 1883.

Charles J. Colonna (1849–1920) founded Colonna's Shipyard in 1875 when he was just 26 years old. Prior to establishing his own business, he served an apprenticeship as a ship's carpenter. The business has been passed down to other generations of the family and is now in its 127th year.

operated yard- and thread-spinning mills. The business moved from Philadelphia to Berkley, where advantages and inducements surpassed those offered by other sections of the country. The aggregate capital of the mills amounted to over $750,000 and more than 1,000 people were employed in them.

The Berkley Daily News, an afternoon newspaper, was owned and edited by E.E. Hathaway and T.F. Humphries. The subscription price was 5¢ a week.

Small, four-wheeled, horse-drawn streetcars were introduced in Berkley on February 3, 1888. Each carried about 20 passengers. The route went from the Berkley Ferry on Chestnut Street to the Belt Line Railroad at Liberty Street. There was a livery stable at either end of the car line, and the car barns were located at Thirteenth and Liberty Streets. The firm of T.H. Synon, William Tillotson & J.H. Norton owned the Berkley Street Railway. The route was later extended to South Norfolk. The streetcar company was required to keep the tracks and surrounding areas clear of any droppings produced by the horses. The driver stood on the front platform and was provided very little protection from the elements. In winter, an effort was made to keep the passengers' feet warm by covering the floor with straw.

In 1894, a Mr. Brown from Delaware took over operation of the Berkley Street Railway and electrified it. Brown had been a lumberman and apparently had a desire to increase his financial holdings in the area. At this time, a new route was established that extended to Norfolk by way of Campostella and Brambleton, both of which had recently been annexed by the City of Norfolk. The terminal for the Berkley Street Railway and Atlantic Terminal Company was located at City Hall Avenue and Atlantic Street in Norfolk.

Competition began when the Norfolk Railway and Light Company started a line in Berkley. The route started at Pearl Street, passed through Walnut, Clifton, and Patrick Streets to Main Street and then down Maple Avenue (which later became West Indian River Road), terminating at the stockyards near the Norfolk & Western Railroad crossing.

The Norfolk County Ferry Company had a contract at that time to run ferryboats to Berkley on a 20-minute schedule. The boats were named the *City of Norfolk* and the *City of Portsmouth*. Later, a third boat, the *Twin City*, was added to provide a 15-minute schedule.

Prior to 1889, the Berkley post office occupied a small frame building on Walnut Street. When the Martin Building was constructed in 1889, it housed the post office, the Chesapeake and Potomac Telephone Exchange, the Berkley Permanent Building and Loan Association, and the offices of the firm of Martin, Tilley & Martin.

By an act of legislature, Berkley was incorporated as a town on March 3, 1890. In the 1890s, the town boasted three box factories, a cigar factory, three foundries and machine shops, six lumber manufacturers, four marine railways, two gristmills, two knitting mills, two weekly newspapers, three shipyards, one electric railway, one telephone exchange (Southern States), one waterworks, one dredging plant, one college, one electric light plant, one chemical works, two creosote plants, one paving block plant, a pipe factory, and numerous stores of all classes.

The first members of the town council were as follows: (ward one) L.B. Allen, W.L. Berkley, A.M. Hawkins, and B.C. Bilisoly; (ward two) C.S. Russell, J.L. Milby, James F. Tatem, and W.H. Kirby; (ward three) Thomas Wininger, Charles W. Parks, and J.J. Ottley. The first meeting was held on the evening of March 18, 1890, in the hall of the Hope Fire Company, which was at the corner of Chestnut Street and the Norfolk & Southern Railroad. The Hope Fire Company was one of the independent firefighting organizations hired to fight any conflagrations that might break out.

Reporting at a later meeting, the Committee on Ordinance and Police thought that the three police officers were sufficient, but that their pay was not enough. The committee recommended that the compensation be raised to $50 per month.

At the meeting of the town council on December 1, 1891, the members awarded a contract to Luke Hughes to keep the street lamps filled with oil and lit. He made his rounds seven evenings a week, and for this, he received the sum of $92.50 per month. Prior to the installation of street lamps, anyone wanting to go out at night carried a lantern.

In May 1896, electricity became available to Berkley through the Berkley Electric Light and Power Company, which had a capacity of 100 arc lights and 600 incandescents. The company entered into a contract with the town to furnish between 40 and 50 arc lights, and subscription for its incandescent service was well received by the public.

The financial institutions of Berkley included the Berkley Permanent Building and Loan Association, which was organized in 1886. Its first officers were Marcellus Miller (president), P.H. Broulett (vice president), Charles S. Wood (secretary), and J.J. Ottley (treasurer). The directors were Marcellus Miller, J.J. Ottley, Alvah H. Martin, J.M. McDonough, P.H. Broulett, Charles S. Wood, B.C.

This 1895 picture of the ferry was taken at the Norfolk & Southern terminal. The town of Berkley is in the background and several tall ships are docked on the waterfront.

Bilisoly, John M. Berkley, C.S. Russell, James L. Milby, Parke Poindexter, and G.O. Williams. On December 5, 1894, the Atlantic Permanent Building and Loan Association was organized.

The Chesapeake Building Association, which was originally the Chesapeake Classified Building Association, was founded in 1895. Early officers were Foster Black (president), Edward Munro Tilley (vice president), Samuel Bland (treasurer), and George Tilley (secretary). The board of directors was composed of the listed officers and J.J. Ottley, Alvah H. Martin, E.F. Fruit, William Tillotson, and Sam W. Wilson. George Martin served as the association's attorney.

On April 1, 1900, Alvah H. Martin organized the Merchant and Planters Bank with the beginning capital of $30,000. The first officers were Foster Black (president), Alvah H. Martin (vice president), George Tilley (cashier), and George Martin (attorney). The first directors were Alvah H. Martin, Foster Black, William M. Tilley, W.L. Berkley, J.H. Jacocks, J.J. Ottley, William Tillotson, W.B. Daugherty, and E.F. Fruit.

Garrett & Company Winery was established in 1835 in St. Louis, Missouri. In 1903, Paul Garrett opened a branch in Berkley at the foot of Chestnut Street. Virginia Dare, a popular wine of the day, was manufactured at the Berkley plant. Garrett operated the business until Prohibition forced him to close in 1916. The winery, which had been very prosperous, had provided employment to many Berkley residents. Many citizens felt that Prohibition was responsible for the Great Depression, which followed some years later.

In 1917, during World War I, the Imperial Tobacco Company, under the management of John A. Moore, began storing tobacco in warehouses in the

Norfolk area. It purchased Garrett's Winery for some of this storage space, and this later became the Imperial Docks. The Imperial Docks were leveled on April 4, 1919, by a fire that started on the fifth floor.

In the latter 1700s, a drawbridge was located at one end of what would become South Main Street. This bridge, which connected Washington to Norfolk, served as a means of thoroughfare for carriages. The property leading to the bridge was part of the Herbert plantation and had been donated to the community by the Herbert family. The Norfolk & Western Railroad Company complained that the bridge interfered with the traffic of large boats going to their grain elevator, so the company bought the bridge, obtained a permit from the state government, and had it removed in 1881. After removal of the old drawbridge, a foot ferry, which was operated by E.L. Bell, was established at that location and remained active until the Berkley Bridge was built in 1916.

Ben Tatem, chief magistrate for Norfolk County, was one of the operators of another foot ferry that ran from the end of Chestnut Street to Norfolk and Portsmouth. People wanting to shop in Norfolk would leave their carriages on property owned by the local tavern and travel across the river in one of the small passenger boats. Later, steam-operated ferries were used. Because there was an abundance of wood from the local lumber mills, slab wood was burned in the furnaces of the early steamboats.

As early as 1636, Norfolk County had a ferry system. By 1637, there were three established ferries in Lower Norfolk County. They were supported by a levy of 6 pounds of tobacco. In 1702, the fare from "Norfolk Towne" to "Sawyer's Point" in Portsmouth was 6 pence for a man and 1 shilling for a man and horse.

The Berkley Bridge, which was built in 1916, extended from South Main Street in Berkley to East Main Street in Norfolk. It was privately owned and therefore

The Berkley Bridge, which was built in 1916, extended from South Main Street in Berkley to East Main Street in Norfolk. In 1952, a new bridge-tunnel complex went into operation and shortly thereafter this old bridge was removed.

required payment of a toll from each passenger crossing it, even those riding the streetcar. A toll collector would collect 2¢ from each commuter. In 1946, the City of Norfolk bought the bridge and discontinued the toll. In May 1952, a new bridge from Berkley to Norfolk and a tunnel to Portsmouth went into operation. The old bridge was eventually removed, and the streetcars were replaced with buses. After operating for more than 300 years, the ferries ceased operation.

In February 1898, Frey and Armstrong would saw, split, and deliver a cord of hard wood for $5, slab wood and board ends for $3 per cord, and five cord lots could be purchased for $2.50 a cord. Charles E. Scott & Co. delivered a $3 cord of slab wood for $2.50 on Tuesday or Thursday of each week.

The office for Tilley's Lumber Mills was located at 288 Water Street in Norfolk. The business was begun in 1873 under the firm name of Hunter & Tilley. In 1883, E.M. Tilley became the sole owner, and in 1896, his son William took over management of the mills. The Tilleys owned an additional 10 acres on the Southern Branch of the Elizabeth River adjoining the mills.

The Bank of Berkley was established under private state license in 1897 and was owned and managed by R.W. Brooks. Brooks was born and raised in Baltimore, but moved to Virginia in 1886, where he married and made his home. He was 33 when he opened the business. The institution was of much benefit and convenience to local interests. It was more accessible than those of nearby Norfolk, and banking hours were much longer—the bank remained open until 7 o'clock in the evening and 8 o'clock Saturday night.

R.B. Mercer operated a blacksmith and wheelwright establishment on Main Street near Berkley Avenue. He served a term of nearly five years in an apprenticeship under a leading blacksmith in Suffolk, Virginia. Just eleven days before his term was to expire, his employer heard of an opening at Richmond and released him from his contract so that he could accept the position. After spending five years in Richmond, Mercer moved to Berkley and opened a shop.

One of the most progressive businesses in Berkley was the firm of C. Bliven, Son & Company. For 15 years, Charles Bliven was one of the leading dock builders in Tidewater Virginia. Around 1897, he built a modern coal elevator and water supply station near the Berkley ferry landing. The pier was situated opposite the central portion of Norfolk and near the business section of Berkley and was in close proximity to a number of machine shops and ship chandlers' stores. The senior member of the firm was also superintendent of the Berkley water work.

The Norfolk Shaving Parlor, located at 353 Main Street, advertised first-class work at popular prices. A gentleman could get a shave for 5¢, hair cut for 10¢, shampoo for 10¢, and a singe for 10¢. An expert bootblack was always in attendance. In 1898, the belief was that a respectable gentleman's appearance could only be maintained by good barbering.

At the foot of Main Street in Berkley were the shipyards of L.C. Jones, a gentleman of experience as a shipbuilder and repairer. Part of the equipment of those yards, which covered over 2 acres, was a marine railway of three sections with traction power enough to draw up vessels of 200 tons register.

Jones was a native of the area and served on the local council and several committees. He believed that the best interests of Portsmouth, Norfolk, and Berkley were so closely allied that the three locations would eventually become one corporation. This did not occur, however, because the City of Norfolk annexed the Town of Berkley in 1906 and Portsmouth is still an independent city.

Among the most enterprising businessmen of Berkley was George T. Tilley, who operated one of the leading real estate and insurance businesses of Berkley. His office was located at 4 Berkley Avenue. Tilley was also the secretary of two successful building and loan businesses, the Chesapeake Building Association and the Berkley Permanent Building and Loan Association.

One of the longest established business enterprises in Berkley was that of Captain Joseph Baker. This business was founded by Captain Joseph Baker and, subsequent to his death, was carried on by Captain G.K. Baker. After G.K. Baker's death, his widow entrusted the business to Captain W.H. Kirby and then to P.M. Pritchard. The Baker estate not only consisted of a machine shop, but also towing, dredging, and pile-driving businesses. The machine shop was located near the Norfolk & Southern Railroad.

In November 1897, G.A. Thompson & Son opened a new drugstore in the fashionable residential district on Berkley Avenue. It was fitted in native woods, was stocked with everything in the drug line, and included a handsome new soda fountain. The business style of the firm read, "G.A. Thompson and Son, Manufacturing Chemists and Physicians' Supplies." G.A. Thompson was a graduate of the Chicago College of Pharmacy, and his son B.J. Thompson was a

The Berkley Machine Works and Foundry manufactured this motor car. The business is still operating near Interstate 464 and the Berkley Bridge.

graduate of the Ada Pharmaceutical College of Ada, Ohio. Both father and son had previously been in the drug business in Newhaven, Virginia, but decided to move to Berkley, where superior advantages could be realized.

In later years, the Rex Theatre operated next to the drugstore. To attract business, one night during the week, each theatre patron received a piece of glassware. Mr. Steingold operated a dry goods store in the same vicinity.

W.L. Berkley & Company, a leading furniture and stove dealer, occupied the Waverly Building. The stock embraced a large line of furniture and stoves at prices that could be afforded by the wealthy and the poor. The merchandise was sold for either cash or on an installment plan. Waverly L. Berkley, son of town founder Lycurgus Berkley, was head of the firm. Other furniture stores in Berkley were those of A.J. Legum, Louis Legum, and J.W. Legum. A.J. eventually moved from 805 Liberty Street to Church Street in Norfolk.

T.H. Bond operated a wheelwright shop on Chestnut Street near Berkley Avenue. Originally from Nansemond County, Bond started the business in September 1897.

Samuel G. Jones and Z.B. Jones operated Berkley Machine Works and Foundry. The docks were at Fort Lee and Elizabeth Streets. The shops were at the foot of Mulberry Street. It has been said that Samuel Jones was a stiff, proper man who wore a necktie at all times. As the story goes, a farm equipment salesman visited his office one day without a tie, and Jones promptly opened his desk drawer where he had a collection of ties, asked the man to select one, put it on, and never come into his office again without one. The story had a happy ending—Jones bought the piece of farm equipment. Other machine shops in Berkley were those owned and operated by Jim Burton and Phillip Richard. Burton had worked for Colonna's Shipyard as a machinist.

Berkley's location on the Elizabeth River was responsible for the large number of shipyards and other water-related industries in the area. There were several lighterage companies operating along the river (a lighter was a flat-bottom barge used in transporting goods to ships). Among them was the Norfolk Lighterage Company, owned by Captain Edwin A. Phelps. Captain Phelps served as harbor master, tugboat captain, and later became captain of the tug *Seaboard*, which was owned by the Seaboard Railroad.

BERKLEY EDUCATION

The public schools of Berkley were in the Washington District of Norfolk County. E.M. Tilley, M.C. Keeling, and T.W. Butt were members of the Norfolk County School Board. One of the early teachers was a man named Simmons, and his pupils referred to him as "Puss" Simmons. A little later came Miss Sue Parker and Miss Rosa Parker, and they taught in the two-room school on Walker Avenue between Fifth and Sixth Streets. When Miss Annie Gammon came to teach, another room was added to the building. Other rooms were added as needed, and later a brick building became the school's permanent home.

The Reverend Doctor Robert Gatewood was a chaplain in the Confederate army. He served as associate pastor of St. Paul's Church in Norfolk, and when St. Paul's Episcopal Church was built in Berkley in 1872, he became its pastor. Reverend Gatewood's home was behind the church, beside the school where he taught small groups of local children.

Prior to 1900, the Berkley public schools were under the direction and supervision of O.L. Kennedy. Professor Kennedy served as the principal for the George Washington School and was assisted by 6 teachers to instruct approximately 330 pupils.

On old Liberty Street, just beyond where the Belt Line train crossed, was a school attended by students who lived in the "McCloud Town," "Bloodthirsty," and "Sweet Canaan" communities. Among the first educators there were George W. Braye (principal) and a Mr. Johnson and his wife.

The City of Norfolk annexed Berkley in 1906. Soon after this, the Abraham Lincoln School on old Eighth Street was opened. John Riley Dungee and Eugene Southall were among the first principals to serve the school.

The Robert Gatewood School on Poplar Avenue in Hardy Homestead opened in 1912. It was named for Reverend Robert Gatewood, a clergyman and former headmaster at the Norfolk Academy. Among the early teachers were Miss Margaret Borden (first grade), Miss Louisa Tatem, and Miss Hannah Warren. The school, which stood on the avenue lined with poplar trees, closed in the 1970s and was torn down in the 1990s.

The area's many private schools were well patronized until about 1900, when the progress of public education made private secondary schools almost unnecessary. Among the early private institutions were those operated by William P. Jones (who at one time was mayor of Berkley), Mrs. Parron, and Harriet Godfrey. These three institutions were located in the Montalant section. Miss Berry Carnes taught on Mulberry Street and then on Chestnut Street. Later,

Reverend Roger Charnock opened a school in the old courthouse building at Walnut and Pine Streets. Professor W.B. Loving's school was situated on Maple Avenue, which was later renamed Indian River Road.

Ryland Institute was incorporated by an act of the General Assembly of Virginia on January 11, 1892. It was a private institution founded by Miss Lula M. Butt and was conducted by her until the close of the 1896–1897 school year. Miss Pauline R. Larrabee, a native of Port Allegany, Pennsylvania, who had served as Miss Butt's first assistant for a period of three years, then leased the school. Its avowed purpose was to provide young ladies with "excellent facilities for securing liberal culture at reasonable rates, and to develop womanly gifts and graces by the best methods within reach." The school was non-sectarian, but devotional exercises were held each morning and an attempt was made to impress religious truths and obligations upon the minds of the students.

The institution was under the general management of the principal, who was assisted by an efficient corps of teachers, all of whom resided in the main building and devoted their entire time to the school. There was an atmosphere of quiet elegance and refinement about the school, which impressed the visitors and rendered it a charming home to the young ladies who were domiciled therein.

Members of the faculty and the branches of knowledge imparted by them were as follows: Mrs. Lugena E. Larrabee supervised the home department; Miss Pauline R. Larrabee, a graduate of the New England Conservatory of Music, taught harmony, piano, voice, theory, history of music, and pipe organ; Mrs. W.B. Anderson, the preceptress, taught history and mental and moral philosophy; Reverend C.W. Duke, a graduate of Richmond College and Southern Baptist Theological Seminary in Louisville, Kentucky, instructed the Greek classes; Miss Susy Q. Hundley, a graduate of Hollins Institute, instructed Latin, French, German, and mathematics; Miss Almeda R. Larrabee, of West Chester, Pennsylvania, instructed English literature, elocution, rhetoric, and physical culture; Miss Sarah Kinnie Haukins, a graduate of Ryland, instructed the preparatory and intermediate departments in general branches and taught arithmetic in all grades; Miss Clara J. Omsted, of the New England Conservatory, provided instruction in piano and harmony; Miss M. Estelle Butt was in charge of the primary department; Miss Elizabeth Slaymaker was in charge of the art department; Lawrence Larrabee was in charge of the library; Reverend C.W. Duke and Reverend R.M. Chandler officiated as chaplains of the institute; and the attending physicians were three of the leading doctors of Berkley, Drs. F.M. Morgan, E.F. Truitt, and J.C. Norfleet.

BERKLEY'S ECCLESIASTICAL TRADITION

In 1870, there was only one church in Berkley, and that was the Christian Church on South Main Street; Reverend Stephen Barrett served as its pastor. By this time, several Methodist families had settled in the area, and because of the distance and inconvenience in reaching the churches of which they were members, they decided to form a society and make arrangements for regular church services closer to home. A room was secured in the old courthouse, fitted up for religious services, and called the chapel. Methodist ministers of Norfolk and Portsmouth preached on Sunday afternoons.

The church was formally organized by the Reverend A.G. Brown, presiding elder of the Norfolk District. He met with the society in the chapel and the church was organized on November 5, 1870. The first official roll was H.C. Cheatham, preacher in charge, and stewards H.B.C. Walker, M.C. Keeling, H.V. Moore, C.S. Rogers, and Enos Cuthrell. This was the beginning of the Chestnut Street Methodist Episcopal Church, South. Lycurgus Berkley donated a suitable lot at the corner of Chestnut and Payne Streets. The brick church was dedicated on Sunday June 26, 1871, at 11 a.m.

Another new building constructed of granite and sandstone was built at the corner of East Berkley Avenue and First Street (now Dinwiddie Street) in 1900. The congregation moved in on December 16, 1900, and the church changed its name to Memorial Methodist Church. This building was sold to the Antioch Baptist Church in 1959. The congregation built their next sanctuary at 804 Gammon Road in the City of Virginia Beach, and their first service was held on November 13, 1960.

Reverend Robert Gatewood (1829–1909), who served as a chaplain in the Confederate Army during the Civil War, as a headmaster of Norfolk Academy, and as an associate pastor of the old St. Paul's Church in Norfolk, revived the work of the Episcopal Church in Berkley. The Episcopalians living in Berkley had

This painting depicts the Berkley Avenue Baptist Church, which was formed in 1873 but had no permanent home until 1886.

This photograph of the Central Baptist Church in Berkley was taken on Friday, April 14, 1922, the day after the fire that destroyed more than one-third of the town. The church was rebuilt, complete with a new steeple.

first attended church at St. Paul's in Norfolk, but due to the inconvenience of having to cross the river by boat, they decided to form a mission in Berkley. For years, they shared the old county courthouse at the corner of Walnut and Pine Streets with members of the local Methodist Church. Lycurgus Berkley donated a site for the erection of an Episcopal church, which was completed in February 1872. In 1911, the Episcopalians built another church in Berkley at the southwest corner of Dinwiddie Street and Poplar Avenue and named it St. Brides. At that time, they vacated the church that had been built in 1872. The congregation remained in the new church until 1960, when they left Berkley and built St. Brides Church on Sparrow Road in what is now Chesapeake.

In September 1873, the Berkley Avenue Baptist Church was formed. The first pastor was the Reverend J.T. Deans of Churchland. During his two-year pastorate, he regularly rowed a boat across the Elizabeth River to meet with his congregation in Berkley. According to an announcement in the *Norfolk Landmark* on Monday, September 16, 1878, the congregation held a fair and feast at Bowden's Hall, located at the corner of Berkley Avenue and Main Street. The article stated that the church had been meeting in a rented house for five years. A lot at the corner of Berkley Avenue and Liberty (Walnut) Street had been donated for a church building in 1875 by Lycurgus Berkley Sr., but due to a lack of funds, it had not been built. The proceeds from the gala affair went towards the building fund. The church was finally built in 1880, but four years later, it burned. The congregation raised money to rebuild and deposited it in a local bank. In April 1885, the bank failed and the church lost its money. The people struggled again to raise funds for rebuilding, which was accomplished in 1886.

In the early 1900s, the Catholics of Berkley had no local meeting place. Some traveled the distance to the chapel located at old St. Vincent Hospital on Church Street in Norfolk. Others attended services held at St. Mary's of the Immaculate Conception, St. Paul's in Portsmouth, or later on the training ship *Richmond*, which was located at St. Helena Naval Station.

A group of Catholics banded together to see if plans could be made to build a chapel in Berkley. Two people with an intense interest in the project were Mrs. Ella Wood and Mrs. Annie Miller Smith. Wood donated a tract of land in a section known as Hardy Avenue. Smith's godfather, Matthew Dugan, had planned to leave her a substantial inheritance, and at her request, he donated $3,000 toward construction of the chapel. Another donation was received from Fountaine Ryan, a railroad executive. Oyster suppers and chicken dinners were held at the Redmen's Hall in Berkley and Annie Miller Smith conducted lawn parties at her home. These were some of the means used to raise the remaining amount needed for construction of the Catholic chapel.

In 1907, the chapel was built on Hardy Avenue in Berkley. It was dedicated in 1908 and given the name St. Matthew's, in honor of Matthew Dugan. From 1908 until 1924, St. Matthew's was a mission of St. Mary of the Immaculate Conception of Norfolk, whose priests served at great hardship and discomfort.

For many of those years, travel from Norfolk to Berkley was by way of ferry or rowboat across the icy waters of the Elizabeth River. In 1924, Father Michael J. Hartigan became the first resident pastor of St. Matthew's. By 1949, St. Matthew's had outgrown the small church on Hardy Avenue and a search began for land on which to build. Thirteen acres were purchased in Sherry Park; however, ground for the new church was not broken until November 1959. On Trinity Sunday, June 12, 1960, Bishop John J. Russell dedicated the building.

In the early 1900s, the Armstrong Memorial Presbyterian Church was located on South Main Street. It was from this church that the First Presbyterian Church of South Norfolk was organized. After Bowden's Hall was removed, the land was used as a small park. Between 1912 and 1913, a Confederate monument (minus the usual statue) was placed in the center of the park. The sponsors could never afford a statue for the top. An old cannon was mounted near the statue. The place became a hangout for tobacco-chewing Confederate veterans and others that enjoyed sitting on benches beneath the chinaberry trees and passing the time of day. The monument, still minus a statue of Johnny Reb, has been moved from its original site in Berkley and now graces a new location in Norfolk at the Elmwood Cemetery.

BERKLEY'S JEWISH COMMUNITY

The story of Berkley would not be complete without inclusion of the history of the Jewish community. Many of its members became successful merchants, businessmen, or professionals. The first permanent Jewish resident in Norfolk, or possibly southeastern Virginia, was Moses Myers, the son of Haym Myers of

Amsterdam. Moses arrived in 1787 with his wife and his business partner, Samuel Myers. Shortly thereafter, Berkley entered into the Jewish history of Tidewater.

It began with two major developments: the establishment of the first Jewish cemetery for Norfolk-area Jews and, seven decades later, the beginning of East European Orthodox Jewry in the area. Ultimately, Berkley became one of the most close-knit Orthodox Russian-Jewish communities in America.

By 1815, Solomon Marks Jr. and brothers Abraham B. and Solomon B. Nones had established the firm of Marks, Nones & Company in Norfolk. In the same year, Solomon Marks Jr. purchased approximately 5 acres of land near the Herbert home in Washington Point (later known as Berkley). In 1819, Marks's business partner Solomon Nones died, thus creating a need for a Jewish cemetery. He was buried on a section of the property belonging to Marks.

On March 6, 1820, Moses Myers, Benjamin Nones, and Philip I. Cohen bought a 40-foot-wide section of land on the Elizabeth River in Washington Point to be used for a Jewish cemetery. It was an ideal location because it was far enough from the busy city of Norfolk, but still could easily be reached by way of the ferry. In 1821, Moses Myers's son Abram died and was buried there. It is not known if Moses Myers himself was buried in the cemetery at Washington Point when he died in 1835; no marker was ever found and no Jewish cemetery existed in Norfolk at that time. Although a Jewish cemetery was established in Norfolk in 1850, even after this, some Norfolk Jews continued to use the cemetery at Washington Point. When Berkley became a town in 1890, the town council ordered the removal of the cemetery. In approximately three-quarters of a century, only about a dozen bodies had been buried there.

When Lycurgus Berkley came to Washington in 1850, he began developing the point and laying out a town. It was not until 1870 that major industries, mainly lumber and marine, began to come to the area, which by then had become known as Berkley. The economic growth that followed attracted many new residents to Berkley, among them were Jewish immigrants.

In the 1870s, Baltimore was a major port of entry, and the immediate area became overcrowded with Jewish immigrants. The desire to leave led many of them to Berkley, where there were better jobs and less-crowded conditions.

In the early 1880s, Jewish immigrants Abe Legum and his wife, Annie Balser Legum, arrived in Berkley and settled on Liberty Street, which was then a country road. Soon after, Abe's brother Isaac Legum came, and Nathan Abramson followed him. Nathan and Isaac became partners in a dry goods store. About the same time, Moses Salsbury came and set up his business. Other immigrants followed. On November 1, 1890, Davis Glasser bought a building. This was just six days before his wife and four children arrived at the port of entry in Baltimore.

The Legums were from the town of Ligum, Lithuania. Salsbury's name has been said to come from Salisbury, Maryland, where he worked as a peddler. Glasser, whose Hebrew name was "Dovid," used the name Davis for business purposes, perhaps.

The first two generations of the Glasser family in America included Davis and his wife, Sarah Frances Sherman Glasser, and their children: Moses Aaron Glasser, Robert Daniel Glasser, Bessie Glasser Yavner, Louis J. Glasser, Ida May Glasser Caplan, and Annie Glasser Adelstone (the latter two of whom were born in the United States).

In 1902, Moses A. Glasser married Rachel Salsbury at Liberty Hall in Berkley. They eventually raised 10 children. Moses Glasser operated a pawnshop at 930 Liberty Street. The original Mikro Kodesh Synagogue was located on Eleventh Street behind Glasser's pawnshop.

Many grocer and dry goods merchants settled on Liberty Street in Berkley, where they lived and worked. In earlier years, Liberty Street, a country dirt road, ran from the Norfolk County Courthouse to Great Bridge. It has been said that Liberty Street got its name because it began at the courthouse.

By 1889, the community had enough adult Jewish males for a minyon (a quorum of 10 is required by Jewish law to be present to conduct public prayers). The first service was held at Jacob Salsbury's store on Liberty Street. The first Jewish congregation in Berkley was called "Mikro Kodesh." It is possible that it took its name from the Baltimore synagogue of the same name. In February 1892, the congregation purchased land for its Orthodox cemetery. In May 1892, the removal of all the bodies in the original Hebrew cemetery took place. This was the cemetery that had been bought in 1820 by Moses Myers, Benjamin Nones, and Philip Cohen.

On May 12, 1892, the tombstones were removed to the Jewish cemetery in Norfolk. They were all placed in one section and an iron fence was erected to enclose the lot. In July 1892, the first Orthodox Jew was buried in the new Berkley Jewish cemetery. The woman, Celia Kirstein of Portsmouth, was buried in an above-ground tomb. Three months later, a 20-year old Jewish woman from Nansemond County was also buried in the Berkley cemetery.

Berkley's first Orthodox Jewish wedding took place on June 27, 1893, when Fannie Salsbury and Abe Zedd were married. The wedding was attended by both the Jewish and Gentile communities and was well publicized in the local newspaper. At that time, Berkley did not have a synagogue building nor did the congregation have its own rabbi—a rabbi from Norfolk performed the ceremony. Eventually, the Mikro Kodesh Synagogue was erected at Eleventh Street. In 1922, a new structure was erected at the corner of Rockingham and Liberty Streets in Berkley. The building still stands.

BERKLEY FIRE OF 1922

On Thursday, April 13, 1922 (the day before Good Friday), more than a third of Berkley was wiped out by fire. Some sources reported that the blaze started in one of the sheds at the abandoned Tunis Lumber Mill, when an illegal liquor still exploded. The mill, which was located on the Southern Branch of the Elizabeth River, at the extreme south end of Main Street, had not been occupied in nearly six years. It was originally operated as a box factory and planing mill. In the early days of World War I, the property was sold to the Western Electric Company. There was talk that the company was going to erect a manufacturing plant on the site; however, this did not happen. The plant had been stripped of machinery, but the power plant, the planing shop, and a large lumber shed, covering about an acre, were left standing.

The blaze started late Thursday afternoon and spread rapidly to the Tunis docks, where four ships of the Buxton Line were anchored. These craft, the *Watch Hill* (a gas boat), the *Rosedale* (a sidewheel steamer), the *Buxton* (a tug), and the *Martha Stevens* (a freighter), were burned to the water's edge. It was estimated that the loss of the ships would exceed $50,000. A statement from the headquarters of the Buxton Line indicated that the loss of the ships would not interfere with the regular traffic between Norfolk and Richmond.

It was a very windy day, and this caused the flames to spread rapidly from the docks to three ancient brick houses at the end of Main Street, near the St. Helena reservation. Two of the houses were destroyed, and the third one, formerly owned by George G. Martin, was badly damaged but not totally ruined. The wind swept flaming shingles through the air. They landed on the roofs of houses on Culpepper Street and also ignited three small frame buildings on Russell Avenue directly behind the Tunis plant. Sparks were carried by a wind that was continuously changing direction. The houses at the lower end of Craig and

Whithead & Hoag Company of Newark, New Jersey made this fancy badge for the chief of the Berkley fire department. The picture on the badge shows an early horse-driven fire engine that was probably manufactured in the late 1860s.

Middlesex Streets were two-story frame structures built close together. In about a half hour's time, the flames had razed the block and were heading northward, making a path approximately three blocks wide and 1 mile long all the way to Berkley Avenue.

The Ashley Spinning Mills, at the corner of Craig and Louisa Streets, were destroyed. The two-story building had been equipped with valuable machinery. The plant, which had been closed for several months, sustained damages of approximately $75,000. The Central Baptist Church on Walker Avenue at Craig Street, erected 15 years earlier at a cost of $60,000, was totally destroyed. An estimate to replace the church was placed at $100,000.

The Liberty Street business district was totally engulfed in flames. Firefighters from all the surrounding communities were called in to fight the flames. Damages to the buildings and stock of stores on Liberty Street between Craig and Culpepper Streets were estimated at $200,000. Twenty businesses were wiped out or badly damaged in the burned area. Those destroyed or damaged were as follows: Alex Liedman, 800 Liberty Street, building owned by M. Salsbury; Louis Salisbury, 804 Liberty Street, pawn shop, building owned by M. Salsbury; A. Salsberg, 606 Liberty Street, delicatessen shop, building owned by M. Salsbury; J. Yavner, hardware, 808 Liberty Street, owned by occupant; A. Katszowsky, 808 Liberty Street, butcher, building owned by A. Zedd; shoe shop and storage room at 810 Liberty Street, owned by A. Zedd; Zedd Brothers furniture, 812 Liberty Street, building owned by A. Zedd; "colored" barbershop, 814 Liberty Street, building owned by A. Zedd; fruit store, 816 Liberty Street, building owned by A. Zedd; Army and Navy Store, 818 Liberty Street, building owned by A. Zedd; and A. Zedd, soft drinks, building owned by A. Zedd. The buildings and stocks of those businesses were ruined completely.

The store of J.L. Leidman, 900–902 Liberty Street, was damaged by fire and water, as was the "colored" motion picture house at 904 Liberty Street (later known as the Lincoln Theatre), which was operated by W.C. Hartsen and owned by J.R. Legum. On the south side of Liberty Street between Craig and Culpepper Streets, the undertaking establishment of Elis Pendleton was also burned down. The fire required the undertaker to move one body to at least three different locations to avoid an unplanned cremation. This building and also the adjoining one occupied by McCoy Brothers, printers, were owned by Pendleton, and both were destroyed. The shoe shop at 811 Liberty Street, also owned by Pendleton, was destroyed. The other buildings on the south side of the street in the 800 block were tenement houses, and they burned to the ground. Fire or water or both damaged several stores in the 900 block.

The only houses remaining on Craig Street, between Berkley Avenue and Essex Street, were four two-story frame structures on the east side of the street just off Liberty Street. These escaped almost unharmed, although buildings on either side were ruined. The South Norfolk Fire Department concentrated their efforts on this neighborhood.

Sparks were blown by the wind and fell on the Union Stockyards on Maple Avenue extended. The stockyards were next to the plant of the Colonna Marine Railway Corporation on the Eastern Branch of the Elizabeth River. Workmen from Colonna's fought the blaze, thus preventing serious damage. Sparks also fell along the tracks of the Norfolk and Western Railroad, causing a blaze in the weeds and grass for a distance of more than a hundred yards.

By early evening, 500 families were homeless and about 300 houses, stores, and churches had been destroyed. The damage was estimated at $1 million. Also, looting had begun, and eventually the Marines were called in to maintain order.

Admiral Andrews, commandant of the Navy Yard, had cook tents set up at the St. Helena reservation, where food was prepared and the homeless were fed. He also had tents set up to provide shelter for those needing a place to stay.

Through the efforts of city officials and public-spirited citizens, provisions were made to care for most of the refugees in private homes. The admiral, whose first name was not reported in early newspaper accounts, referred to his unoccupied tents as a "peopleless city."

Augustus Stroud, mayor of Titustown, informed City Manager Ashburner of Norfolk that 100 houses in Titustown would be made available to victims of the fire, free of rent, until July 1. Also, two large buildings in Titustown were being converted to commissaries and kitchens where the refugees could be fed. Admiral Andrews of the Navy Yard agreed to furnish as many cots and mattresses as needed. The city manager made arrangements with Meyers & Tabakin furniture store to supply the families with furniture. The furniture could be purchased outright on the installment plan, or could be used temporarily free of charge until the families using it were in a position to rehabilitate their homes.

Mayor Albert Roper of Norfolk expressed the belief that hundreds of the men who lost their homes in the fire would find permanent housing in Titustown and would be given employment at the new municipal terminals that were under construction at the time.

The *Norfolk Ledger-Dispatch* was receiving funds for the relief of those whose home and possessions were destroyed in the fire. A list of contributors, many of them local businesses as well as individuals, appeared in the evening newspaper. The Salvation Army was early on the scene. Arrangements were made to place kettles on the streets of all the local communities, and clothing was collected for distribution. The First Presbyterian Church of Norfolk donated $500, and the Woman's Auxiliary of the Norfolk Presbytery contributed $200. Most of the businesses donated at least $100.

Out of most disasters can be found a story of heroism, and the Berkley fire was no exception. D. Webb, baker third class attached to the collier Orion, entered a burning building on Appomattox Street and rescued three children. After they were safe, he reentered the same building and carried out a baby that was less than a year old. Petty Officer D. Webb was officially commended for risking his life to save the children.

BERKLEY IN THE TWENTIETH CENTURY

The town of Berkley was a short-lived government (only 16 years), and the last meeting of the town council was held on December 19, 1905. George W. Jones presided and the roll call was answered by W.H. Hancock, John C. Simpson, George A. Thompson, J.R. Cunningham, and G.B. Randolph. There was a small group of citizens that were opposed to the annexation. Those who were most outspoken were Mayor L.B. Allen, Dr. E.F. Truitt, and Simon Salisbury.

By order of the Circuit Court of Norfolk County, Berkley became the Eighth Ward of the City of Norfolk on January 1, 1906. Following the annexation, J.O. Wiggs, Berkley's representative to the city council, proposed construction of a bridge from Berkley to Norfolk. Walter H. Taylor drew the plans, but the permit was not granted until 1916.

In 1915, the Berkley Fire Department and Police Station, Station No. 8, which no longer stands, was built on the south side of East Liberty Street near South Main Street. The structure was of brick and stone and contained a tall brick lookout tower at the rear of the building. The fire equipment was horse drawn at that time, and the horses were kept in stalls behind the lower level. The police department occupied the right side of the building.

Pictured here are the members of the 1938 Berkley Boys Club football team. The club was located on Chestnut Street but most of its games were played on this field at St. Helena. Liberty Street is to the left and Berkley Avenue is to the right. At top right are the Rex Theatre and B.J. Thompson's Drug Store. From left to right are (seated) unidentified and Julian Greenough; (kneeling) Mr. Porter, Mr. Merrett, Wayne Irby, Arthur Harriman, Vernon Phelps, Sam Tarkington, Gatewood Deshields, Waverly Wilcox, Mr. Greenough, and Teddy Tarkington; (standing) Mr. Cannon, Max Wilcox, Les Bangs, unidentified, Buddy Briggs, Johnny Baker, Bill Johnson, Buddy Harriman, unidentified, and Dad Blevin (manager).

The Berkley Branch Library was established in a small house at the corner of Patrick and Main Streets on April 20, 1921. Miss Lee Dudley was the librarian.

Berkley had hundreds of businesses and dozens of schoolteachers and doctors. On March 26, 1858, Dr. Robert Stith Bernard Jr. began the practice of medicine at Ferry Point and received his first patient on March 29, 1858. He also opened the first apothecary shop on the Southside, locating it on Chestnut Street near Pine Street. For many years, it was the only drugstore in the area.

Berkley was even the birthplace of Peggy Hopkins Joyce, a well-known actress, who was born on Lee Street in 1893. Joyce had several husbands of great wealth. She died in 1957 at the age of 64.

Even though Berkley was a town of great wealth, in the 1930s, it had its less fashionable neighborhoods. One such neighborhood was Muskrat Row, which was located to the east of State Street, bounded on the north by the Elizabeth River, and centered on Spotico Creek. It was made up of houseboats with no plumbing and the meanest gangs of boys lived there. If a stranger appeared, he was lucky to escape with his life. This area has since been cleared and its former location can be spotted to the left when one crosses the Berkley Bridge from Norfolk.

The town's accessibility to the sea and availability of raw materials attracted Northern capital to the area. Lumber mills, box factories, knitting mills, shipyards, and a large winery were opened along its waterfront. Many of the prominent families of Norfolk made their fortunes on the Southside. Berkley's period of prosperity, however, was temporary. By World War I, the old village at the fork of the Elizabeth River's Eastern and Southern Branches went into decline. Prohibition had put the Garrett Winery out of business. Dwindling forests caused the box factories and lumber mills to leave.

Well-to-do families moved to Norfolk and rented out their large Berkley homes. The homes were divided into apartments and received very little upkeep. The tenants destroyed a large number of these beautiful old homes. Porch railings and pickets were used for firewood. Structures of historic significance were torn down.

Commercial vessels increased in size, making it necessary for their owners to use shipyards that were located on deeper water. St. Helena Naval Training Station was incorporated into the naval station located at Norfolk. To add to all these problems, the fire in 1922 destroyed much of Berkley. A few of the old homes and churches still stand, but most of Berkley has given way to the wrecking ball. There are many acres of empty land. A noticeable change, however, has begun to take place. New residences are starting to pop up on some of the old streets, many of which still carry the names given them by Lycurgus Berkley. Some of the citizens believe that there is hope that Berkley might someday regain part of what has been lost.

5. SOUTH NORFOLK

As time passed, a few of the founding fathers of the village of Berkley decided to acquire land a little farther to the south. After doing so, some of those that had become wealthy from the industries of Berkley began to build large handsome homes in the area that would become South Norfolk.

South Norfolk had its beginning in 1661, when the Southern Branch Chapel of the Church of England was built on a site between Scuffletown Creek and Jones' Creek in the vicinity of present-day Lakeside Park. There were settlers before then, but the opening of the chapel marked the beginning of formal record keeping of events such as births, marriages, and deaths. Many of the original documents are securely stored in the office of the clerk of the Circuit Court of the City of Chesapeake.

The Elizabeth River Parish was divided in 1761, "on account of illegal practises [and] oppressing its inhabitants," according to an act of the assembly. The first election for new vestrymen was held June 6, 1761. The results and number of votes received by each were as follows: John Portlock, 251; Robert Tucker, 250; James Webb, 249; Joshua Corprew, 249; William Smith, 240; Thomas Nash Jr., 239; Samuel Happer, 232; James Wilson, 228; Henry Herbert, 205; John Wilson, 186; Malachi Wilson Jr., 176; and William Happer, 155. John Portlock and William Smith were selected to serve as churchwardens.

As provided in the act of the General Assembly dividing the Elizabeth River Parish, vestrymen of St. Brides Parish sold the land at public auction to John Tucker for 6 pence per acre—172 acres, amounting to 520 pounds and 6 shillings. The deed was dated October 20, 1761. Apparently the land was auctioned to acquire funds to pay parish debts, according to the last entry in the old parish's vestry book: "Here end every Transaction of the Vestry of Elizabeth River Parish till the said Vestry was dissolved and the said Parish was divided into three distinct Parishes."

On August 1, 1763, William Smith and his wife, Ann, conveyed to James Pasteur (minister), John Portlock (churchwarden), and the vestrymen of St. Bride's Parish 200 acres of land in the parish for 350 pounds. Some of the founding fathers of Berkley were responsible for development of the adjacent farmland that became South Norfolk and a number of them built homes in the new village.

This map, which appeared in the February 26, 1898 Berkley edition of the TIPS Weekly *newpaper, served at least two purposes. It advertised the fact that Parke L. Poindexter was a real estate salesman, and it also showed areas of South Norfolk, Berkley, parts of Portsmouth, the U.S. Navy Yard, and other properties.*

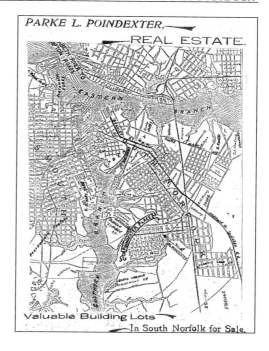

The area that became South Norfolk experienced some settlement during the colonial period but remained rural until the late nineteenth century. The City of Norfolk, located across the Eastern Branch of the Elizabeth River, did not reach its full potential until after the post–Civil War depression, when railroads began to bring coal and produce from the west and south. The new railroads were a boon to Norfolk and also to the farms and villages of Norfolk County. Norfolk's location on the Elizabeth River gave it a prime position for shipping, but prohibited a natural expansion across the river's Eastern Branch. When the railroads came through Norfolk County, they encouraged development all along the line. New industries grew up along the Eastern and Southern Branches of the Elizabeth River and new businesses and houses appeared near the railroad lines.

Prior to 1870, the entire southside was referred to as Berkley or that land near or south of Norfolk. South Norfolk was known as a suburb of Berkley. Although several homes had already been built in the area, some businessmen began to make plans for development of South Norfolk as early as 1889. This land adjacent to Berkley began to be developed with the laying out of streets and building lots. The farm comprising the land between the town of Berkley and what is now Poindexter Street was known as the Green House tract. Alvah H. Martin and others purchased this land for the sum of $3,500, divided it into lots, and put those lots upon the market under the name of Elmsley. Elmsley was that land bounded by Poindexter, Eighteenth, Liberty, and B Streets.

W.S. Butt owned large amounts of land along the Southern Branch of the Elizabeth River in Berkley as well as in South Norfolk between B and D Streets.

Around 1887, there was a foot-bridge across the creek at the end of South Main Street that connected Berkley to the Butt plantation in South Norfolk. Later, the Greenleaf, Johnson Lumber Company purchased a large part of Butt's land.

Development of adjoining land soon followed. Alvah Martin and his wife, Mary, donated two lots, each with 30 feet fronting on Liberty Street and having a depth of 100 feet, to be used for construction of the Liberty Street Methodist Episcopal Church, South. The deed was dated October 13, 1890, and the church, which was the first in South Norfolk, was dedicated in May 1892.

Among the early settlers of the South Norfolk area were Admiral Carter W. Poindexter and his family. The admiral had served in the British Navy, and when he came to the area, he built his home, the "Anchorage," on the waterfront across from the Gosport Navy Yard. The Poindexters had three children, Reginald, Parke, and Bettie. Reginald has been credited with having named the community "South Norfolk" prior to 1890. Poindexter Street was named after the family, and the admiral was responsible for having named most of the other streets in South Norfolk. Among them are Jackson, Rodgers, Decatur, Stewart, Hull, Bainbridge, Perry, Porter, Lawrence, Barron, and Truxton. All of these were named for military officers. Guerriere Street was named for the HMS *Guerriere*, which was captured by Captain Isaac Hull and the crew of the USS *Constitution* during the War of 1812.

Later, the Poindexter family moved from the waterfront to a home on Ohio Street in what is now the 1000 block. The house was two stories with an "A" roof and was painted red. The admiral owned two large sailboats, which he used in his import business. He made trips to the Orient and brought back spices, coffee, tea, and other commodities. On one of his trips to China he brought back a ginkgo tree, which he planted in the front yard of his home on Ohio Street. Although the house has since been moved, the tree is still there along with a magnolia that he planted. Of Chinese origin, the ginkgo has fan-shaped leaves. In the fall of the year, it bears yellow fruit that produces an unpleasant smell and the leaves turn a brilliant gold. A small shoot from the Poindexter tree was planted in the front yard of the house located at 1007 Ohio Street and has since grown to maturity.

Eventually the red house with an "A" roof was removed to 1148 Stewart Street. In 1918, one of the boys in the neighborhood set fire to it, completely destroying the kitchen and dining room, which were built off the back of the house. When the house was repaired, a slanted roof was installed to replace the original roof. The kitchen and dining room were removed at that time. This dwelling, which now serves as a duplex, is probably the oldest home in South Norfolk.

When the Poindexters moved from Ohio Street, they relocated to a house that J.P. Andre Mottu had built on his property in the vicinity of what is today the corner of Rodgers and Jefferson Streets. At that time, Rodgers Street did not extend that far and Jefferson Street did not exist. This very large house sat in a field, which included what are now the 1200 blocks of Rodgers, Decatur, and Stewart Streets and all the land in between. A fence protected the area and the entrance was by way of a gate, which was operated by a man known as Solomon the gatekeeper.

J.P. Andre Mottu had served as consul from Belgium. Upon leaving South Norfolk, he purchased the Colley Farm in Norfolk, which was located in the Atlantic City area on the west side of The Hague, near Christ and St. Luke's Church.

By this time, Carter and Mary Poindexter were deceased, and their son Reginald was living in California. Parke and his sister Bettie were the only occupants of the home. Parke L. Poindexter had engaged in farming for many years, but later turned his attention to the development of industries and land. In addition to the residence, he owned a large amount of property, which was known as "Poindexter Place." Probably his last employment was as a justice of the peace for Norfolk County. His duties included trying minor civil and criminal cases, administering oaths, and solemnizing marriages. His office and courtroom were in the Flatiron Building, which was also referred to by some as the "Berlin Block." This building, which housed all the municipal offices of the local government as well as a movie theater (where for 6¢ one could see a silent film), was located on Liberty Street near the Belt Line Railroad crossing.

Parke Poindexter carried his pistol and a newspaper in a market basket on his arm and rode the streetcar to and from work each day. It has been said that he would stop in the middle of a court session and send a policeman to the saloon, which was in the same building, to fetch him a pitcher of beer. This he would consume while continuing to perform his duties. Parke passed away a few years after the move from Ohio Street, and his sister Bettie followed shortly thereafter. Parke Deans Jr., son of Parke Poindexter and Lucy Saunders Deans, was born on December 13, 1907, and died June 22, 1922, at the age of 14 years and 6 months.

After the passing of the Poindexters, the property was acquired by Jesse Cuthrell, who used it to start a dairy. Each day the cows were driven down Ohio Street almost to the Royster Plant, where they would graze all day and then they were driven back to the barn in late afternoon for milking. At that time, none of the streets in South Norfolk were paved and much of the land was marshy. There was a marsh bordering the dairy, which Cuthrell had dug out so that it would fill up with water from nearby drainage ditches and rainwater. This hole in the ground was filled with 300-pound blocks of ice from John Cuthrell's ice plant and was used as cold storage for the milk. Cuthrell later relocated his dairy to Princess Anne Road in Norfolk.

Around 1916, Jerry G. Bray Sr., O.J. Parker, D.W. Lindsey, and one other person purchased this large piece of property. The men had Rodgers Street extended from Ohio Street, disassembled the large house, divided the property into lots, and sold them. This became known as the Beechwood Tract. Jerry Bray was into contracting, and using the lumber salvaged from the old Mottu/Poindexter house, he was able to build several smaller houses, which are still standing.

By 1900, the area now designated as the historic district of South Norfolk had been divided into housing lots. Although the old County Road continued to run through the district, most of the present streets had been laid out. The section

This drawing depicts the Poindexter home in 1894. In 1918, one of the neighborhood boys set fire to it, destroying the kitchen and dining areas at the back of the house. The house, minus those areas, was rebuilt and now stands in the 1100 block of Stewart Street.

bounded by Park Avenue, the old County Road, and Stewart Street was given the name Quincy Place. It covered a large part of the southern section of the district near where Lakeside Park is today. At one time, this land had been the Quincy farm. In 1900, there were only two houses in Quincy Place.

The Elizabeth Land Improvement Company owned the area bounded by Bainbridge Boulevard and Stewart, Holly, and Poindexter Streets on the western side. The company had laid out streets and lots, but there were no houses on their property, which continued for several blocks to the west. Their land did include the Elizabeth Knitting Mill, which was south of Park Avenue and west of Bainbridge Boulevard.

A triangular-shaped section enclosed by Stewart Street, Park Avenue, and the County Road did not have street and lot divisions, but this section did include a lot (which had a house and outbuilding) owned by J.P. Andre Mottu and three open lots carrying the names "Whitehead," "Tilley," and "Woodard." The Synon and Frost addition was the most developed section in 1900. This contained a large triangular section bounded by the old County Road, Poindexter Street, and Seaboard Avenue. The Baptist church, which was a wooden building, stood at the corner of Guerriere Street and Chesapeake Avenue. Earlier, in August 1891, a two-room wooden school building had been erected on Jackson Street in the middle of the east side of what is now the 1100 block.

Some residential development in South Norfolk had gotten underway prior to 1890, but did not really pick up speed until the 1890s and around 1900. By 1900, the population was almost 1,500. In early 1900, Decatur Street was only one block in length and that was from Buchanan Street to Eighteenth Street. Johnson Park covered the rest of the area up to Poindexter Street. Later, Decatur Street was extended from Poindexter Street to Park Avenue. Chesapeake Avenue terminated at Holly Street, Rodgers Street stopped at Ohio Street, and Hull Street began at Poindexter Street, as it does today, and came to an end at Park Avenue. Stewart Street also came to an end at Park Avenue, and a footbridge was used to cross a creek to Hull Street. A baseball field covered much of the area that is now the 1400 and 1500 blocks of Chesapeake Avenue and a portion of Park Avenue.

Contributing largely to the growth and development of the community was the extension of the Berkley Street Railway from the limits of Berkley to a point at the intersection of Chesapeake Avenue and Guerriere Street. At a later date, the streetcar line extended to the limits of South Norfolk and on to Money Point, which became part of the village of Portlock.

The developers of the Synon and Frost addition were Thomas H. Synon and Daniel E. Frost, real estate developers with offices at 17 Granby Street in downtown Norfolk. Synon was also president of the Berkley Street Railway. It was thought that South Norfolk would become a streetcar suburb; however, for the most part, this did not take place. Most of its residents did not take advantage of the streetcar to ride to work in Berkley or Norfolk. The two railroads that passed through South Norfolk created employment, as did new industries that located along the Southern Branch of the Elizabeth River.

South Norfolk had been laid out into large lots and broad streets, giving it somewhat of an advantage over Berkley, whose lots were, many of them, narrower. These advantages helped to build up South Norfolk and make it the site of nice homes.

The nearby City of Norfolk had an ordinance that required brick construction, but most houses built in South Norfolk were of wood-frame construction. It was the natural choice of the developers, which included E.M. Tilley, owner of the Tilley Lumber Company. Tilley furnished the lumber and his son-in-law John Jones built the houses.

The Tilley home at 1106 Chesapeake Avenue, at the corner of Guerriere Street, was among the first of many stately homes to be built in South Norfolk. Tilley had settled in Berkley after the Civil War, went into the lumber business, and helped in many ways with the founding of Berkley. Construction of Tilley's new home was begun in 1890 and was completed in 1893. It contained 22 rooms and 7 fireplaces. A breezeway was built between the main structure and the kitchen, which was off the back of the house. A stairway in the breezeway lead to the servant quarters over the kitchen. Tilley's stable, behind the house, faced Guerriere Street and his carriage house was located nearby on Jackson Street. In later years, the carriage house was converted into a dwelling and remains so today. The stable was constructed with a wooden floor, and when walking by, the horses would begin stamping, especially in the heat of summer when there were a lot of flies around.

A large drainage ditch ran beside the Tilley property. This ditch continued down to Cuthrell's dairy, branched across Park Avenue, and emptied into a creek. The creek flowed into a spillway that was in the area where Lakeside Park is today. The spillway emptied into Scuffletown Creek, which connects with the Elizabeth River.

The property between E.M. Tilley's home at 1106 Chesapeake Avenue and his son-in-law Jones's house at 1130 Chesapeake Avenue would remain vacant for several years. E.M. Tilley had two other large homes built around the early 1890s. One was situated at 1049 Chesapeake Avenue on the corner diagonally across from his residence. This was for his son George Thomas who had also resided in Berkley. The other house was constructed at 1007 Ohio Street and was for his other son William Munro Tilley.

William M. Tilley eventually took over management of Tilley Lumber Company. His brother, George, worked in his father's business for a while, but later entered the real estate and insurance business. All of the Tilley interests coincided to promote the development of South Norfolk.

In 1873, J.A. McCloud operated the only store in South Norfolk in an area that was then known as McCloudtown. By 1888, S.W. Wilson's grocery store was located in a small frame house on Liberty Street near the Norfolk & Western Railroad. Wilson's capital stock in the business then amounted to $50.

In 1895, Dr. N.G. "Nick" Wilson began the practice of general medicine at the home of his aunt Carrie Edwards on Liberty Street extended. On November 28, 1895, he married Beulah Halstead. They resided in a white house with a white picket fence. This later became 1401 Poindexter Street and was known as Wilson's corner. (In the mid-1930s, Preston's Pharmacy was built at that location.) In 1904, Dr. Wilson built a large handsome house at 13 Chesapeake Avenue.

Around 1900 and 1901, there were a number of other businesses in South Norfolk. On Liberty Street were retail businesses such as confectioners, dry goods merchants, a laundry, an eating house, a fish and oyster dealer, a furniture dealer, and a saloon. John Jackson, a physician, lived at 1041 Chesapeake Avenue, and the Berkley Street Railway Company had its offices at the corner of Avenue C and Thirteenth Street. Miss Rena B. Wright was the principal of the South Norfolk Public School on Jackson Street, and the Reverend Paul Bradley was pastor of the Methodist Church and Samuel Robinson was minister of the South Norfolk Baptist Church. At this early date some industry was already moving into South Norfolk.

The Chesapeake Knitting Mill was located at the corner of Twelfth and B Streets. It covered that area from B Street past where Bainbridge Boulevard is today. This was the dividing line between Berkley and South Norfolk. Around the latter part of the 1930s, the company moved its operation to Martinsville, Virginia. Eventually the main building was torn down; however, the building that was used for boxing and shipping remained and was used by other companies. The S.L. Williams candy factory, which had its beginning on Chestnut Street in Berkley, relocated to this site and remained there until the construction of Interstate 464 forced the removal of the building. The candy company is now located at 1230 Perry Street in South Norfolk.

Before 1920, Sam Creef ran an auto supply store on Poindexter Street, then this Oldsmobile repair and filling station on B and Poindexter Streets. Creef, his wife, Elsie, and a friend are shown here behind the counter in the station's showroom. A Willard brand battery is displayed next to very narrow tires.

The success of the Chesapeake Knitting Mill was the direct cause of the construction of the Elizabeth Knitting Mill. The Elizabeth Knitting Mill was located on land donated by Parke Poindexter west of Bainbridge Boulevard at Park Avenue, where the Rena B. Wright School is now located. Parke Poindexter and E.M. Tilley held large amounts of stock in both mills. Foster Black, who was married to one of E.M. Tilley's daughters, leased the Chesapeake and Elizabeth Mills.

After the death of Foster Black in 1903, William Sloane ran both mills. Many local residents worked in the knitting mills, which manufactured union suits (one-piece long johns). A common sight was the delivery wagon drawn by two white horses carrying crates of union suits to the Norfolk & Western Railway station at Seaboard Avenue and Guerriere Street. These crates were shipped up north where the winters were very cold. In the summer, on the way back to the mill, the driver would stop in the shade of the elm trees on Ohio Street to let the horses cool down and dry.

The front of the Elizabeth Knitting Mill faced Perry Street and the back was near the 1400 block of Porter Street. The structure was torn down about 1933, and in 1934, the bricks were salvaged and cleaned by a group of citizens who were paid according to the number of bricks cleaned. These were used in the construction of individual homes. The following summer, this land was used by a circus; it has been said that flies plagued the entire neighborhood.

William Sloane, like the Tilley and Black families, came from the North after the Civil War, settled in Berkley, and then moved to South Norfolk. William and Florence were married in 1895 and built their home on the corner of Chesapeake Avenue and Ohio Street. Sloane lived at what is now 1203 Chesapeake Avenue with his family and a chauffeur. In 1908, the Sloanes had a summer home (the Hermitage) in the Lochhaven section of Norfolk. Today, this home, located at 7637 North Shore Road, houses the Hermitage Foundation Arts Museum.

By 1902, a thriving community existed where farms and strawberry fields had been just a few years earlier, and the estimated population of South Norfolk was 2,000. One of the most important developments was the processing of seabird droppings, or guano. Farmers learned in the mid-nineteenth century that those droppings made a particularly effective fertilizer. In a busy horse-and-buggy era in Tarboro, North Carolina, a former country boy by the name of Frank Sheppard Royster opened his first fertilizer factory in 1885. In 1891, Royster sent his young protege Charles F. Burroughs Sr. to the area to start up production in a Berkley warehouse.

Soon thereafter, the company built a large fertilizer plant in South Norfolk and operated under the name Columbia Guano Company. In 1898, Royster made Norfolk his permanent headquarters, and on August 2, 1900, changed the firm's name to F.S. Royster Guano Company.

By 1910, the Pocomont Guano Company and A.S. Lee and Sons, lime manufacturers, were also operating on the waterfront. Arthur S. Lee of Richmond, Virginia, had established the firm of A.S. Lee and Sons.

William Sloane, one of the owners of the local knitting mills, had this stately home built on the corner of Chesapeake Avenue and Ohio Street in 1895.

The number of houses continued to increase in South Norfolk. More houses appeared on Chesapeake Avenue and on scattered lots throughout the southern section of the community, although an inlet from the Southern Branch of the Elizabeth River continued to reach as far as the area where Lakeside Park would eventually be located. This inlet was a part of Scuffletown Creek. There were a large number of houses in the blocks bounded by B, D, Eighteenth, and Twenty-second Streets. Seaboard Avenue was probably the most populated of all the streets at the time.

The residents of Seaboard Avenue included workers such as carpenters, grocery merchants, and employees of the local guano, lumber, knitting mill, creosote, and dredging businesses. Most were native born with one exception, Emanuel Price, a house carpenter who had been born in Sweden.

As a note of interest, the two-story house at 1119 Seaboard Avenue had been built around 1910. There were two lots numbered and designated as lots 58 and 59 on the plat of D.E. Frost's property. This house and these lots sold for $1,025 in October 1931.

Among other early residents of South Norfolk were the Funks. A tugboat captain, Captain Funk built his home at 1416 Poindexter Street in 1894. The front of his house was built to resemble the bow of a tugboat. Across the street was the home of George L. Grimes, who was married in Berkley in 1888 and moved to South Norfolk soon after his wedding. At the corner of A and Twenty-second Streets was the Madrin home; this house was occupied later by the Sawyer family, who converted a part of the first floor into a confectionery store.

John Johnson stands behind the counter of the Hitching Post restaurant in Robert Rowland's hotel on Bainbridge Boulevard and Portlock Road.

A group of workers pose in front of Sam Wilson's South Norfolk Market in 1928, most likely in December judging by the Christmas decorations in the windows.

The two-story house directly across the street at the corner of A and Twenty-second Streets belonged to the parents of Bill White. Around 1909, the fire department used it as their first headquarters; by that time, the property on which it stood was at the corner of the schoolyard. The fire department stored their fire hose and reel in a building next to the Madrin house. When the fire department no longer used the building for storing the hose and reel, Jack Brown acquired the property. It was there that Brown stored his horse and cart, which he used to pick-up trash. This was the beginning of trash collection in the village of South Norfolk.

In 1915, the firemen built a new two-story fire station next to Brown's building on Twenty-Second Street, and the house that they vacated became classrooms for the domestic science, or home economic, classes of the South Norfolk school. The sewing classroom consisted of cutting tables, foot-pedal Singer sewing machines, and a pot-bellied stove in the middle of the room. Mrs. Julia Parker was the teacher.

In the meantime, the construction note for the new fire station came due and the department could not raise the necessary funds. The building was put up for sale and was purchased by the Woodmen of the World lodge. It then became known as the W.O.W. Hall. Around the same time, Brown's building was removed and a house was built between the Madrin house and the W.O.W. Hall. This became the residence of Johnny Brinn, who worked for Dean Preston, owner of Preston's Pharmacy. Preston built his own large home at the corner of D and Twenty-second Streets. In later years, Preston moved to Kemp Lane off Indian River Road, and the house in South Norfolk was owned by the Briggs family and then the Overtons.

Sam Wilson, owner of the South Norfolk Market, lived on Poindexter Street. When he purchased a triangular piece of land that was bounded by D, Decatur, and Buchanan Streets, he sold the house on Poindexter Street to the Consolvo family and made plans to build a large home on the newly acquired land. The year was 1907 and construction was underway on the various state houses and buildings that would be featured at the Jamestown Exposition. All the construction workers in the area were employed on that project and none were available to build the new Wilson home. Thus, construction of the house was put on hold and the Wilson family could not move when promised. Eventually some kind of agreement was reached between the two families.

After work on the exposition buildings was nearly complete, Wilson was able to hire a contractor to build his home. Buchanan Street, which ran behind the new Wilson home, was the location of the garage, and Wilson's horse and delivery wagon were housed there when the store was not open. The area also included a rose garden, fig trees, and a playhouse. The playhouse was an ideal place for one of the Wilson boys and his friends to congregate and play poker. When his father discovered this, the building was demolished. The address of the home was 64 D Street; it still stands but the address has changed to 604 D Street.

Dr. Frank Wilson and his wife, Ruth, lived on Chesapeake Avenue across the street from his brother Dr. Nick Wilson (the doctors were not part of Sam Wilson's family). Sometime after 1914, Frank bought his brother's home at 13 Chesapeake Avenue, where he practiced general medicine until January 1919. He then sold the house to J.R. Williams, who moved his funeral business from Chestnut Street in Berkley to the large home on Chesapeake Avenue in South Norfolk.

Josey C. Brothers, superintendent of one of the knitting mills, lived on Seaboard Avenue before moving to 1035 Chesapeake Avenue. After Dr. Jackson moved, Dr. T.B. Wood acquired the large home at 1041 Chesapeake Avenue. In later years, it was divided into apartments and given the name "Carver Hall." William Lane lived across the street at 1044 and his brother James Thomas Lane, owner of J.T. Lane's Drug Store on Liberty Street, lived next door at 1050. These homes were built around 1895.

In the 1890s, as mentioned earlier, E.M. Tilley constructed a house at 1049 Chesapeake Avenue for his son George Thomas Tilley. The barn, or carriage house, was located behind the home and faced Guerriere Street. After the Tilleys, Robert B. Rowland lived there with his wife, two sons, and two servants. At that time, the carriage house became outfitted with two new Cadillac cars. Rowland was in the fertilizer business and was among the rich and famous of South Norfolk. In later years, he built a home off Indian River Road on Kemp Lane.

In 1893, the South Norfolk Baptist Church was constructed on the corner of Chesapeake Avenue and Guerriere Street in what became the 1100 block. It was a small wooden building, which burned on June 13, 1914. Thomas Black, brother of Foster Black, lived next to the church, and his home sustained damages from this fire in the amount of $250.

Some of the other residents of the 1100 block included the Ambrose family; the Reverend Richard B. Scott, pastor of the Methodist Church; Joe Forbes, a streetcar motorman; the McHorney family; the Abotts; Waverly T. Lane; and the VanVleeks. The home at 1126 Chesapeake was, for several years, the office of Dr. G.W. Simpson. John W. Jones, son-in-law of E.M. Tilley, lived at 1130 in a home built his home around 1888. Glenn R. Leroy, a retail merchant, resided at 1138 and he and Mrs. Leroy converted the front of their home into a store. The local residents referred to it as the "Little Store." Thomas Wininger, who lived at 1137, was also a retail grocery merchant. William B. Ashburn, a physician, had his office in the small house at 1140, and his residence was next door at 1144. Dr. Ashburn had graduated from medical school in Virginia and practiced in South Norfolk until his death in 1923. His son Horace Godwin Ashburn who established his clinic at 1301 Ohio Street in 1927, succeeded him. T.B. Wood, another physician, and Dr. J.O. Belcher, a dentist, both had offices in the same building. After E.M. Tilley died on December 21, 1917, his home at 1106 Chesapeake Avenue was occupied by Q.C. Davis Jr. and his family.

In 1919, a large three-story building was constructed at 1 Chesapeake Avenue by Dean Preston. Also in 1919, the Grand Theatre opened and the large vacant lot at the corner of Chesapeake Avenue and Ohio Street became the location of the Chesapeake Pharmacy and apartments.

Ed Reass operated the Grand Theatre from 1919 until October 1945. At that time he sold the theater to the Visulite Corporation and retired. Around 1970, the Visulite Corporation sold it to Ernie Price. At the end of 1976, Price closed the

This convertible filled with happy young women was part of the fire prevention parade on Chesapeake Avenue in November 1962. It was the end of the road for the parade though, as South Norfolk became part of the city of Chesapeake just two months later. The large white columns on the corner belong to the South Norfolk Baptist Church, and the large house in the background is 1049 Chesapeake Avenue.

theater. It was then acquired by Billy Taylor, who made an effort to revive burlesque entertainment in the Tidewater. A fire, apparently purposely set, scorched the rear of the theater. Taylor himself extinguished the fire after it burned an area 8 to 10 feet wide outside the building and touched the rear door. A considerable amount of kerosene was found in the grass at the rear of the building, and an empty apple cider jug, which smelled of kerosene, was found nearby. Taylor smelled the smoke about 7:15 p.m. and rushed out with a fire extinguisher; after having put the fire out, he remarked that the fire would have no effect on his effort to open a burlesque house.

City Sergeant John R. Newhart, with a court injunction in hand, closed the theater just as the second performer of the evening was getting down to bare facts. Taylor spoke to the audience of 39 men and 3 women and told them that they would have to leave. He then refunded their money.

Farther down to the 1200 block of Chesapeake Avenue near the corner of Ohio Street was the large home of Foster Black (his home would later serve as the parsonage for the Methodist Church). After Black died in 1903, this property became the home of Louie Furman. It is now the location of the Chesapeake Avenue United Methodist Church.

Across the street from Black was the residence of William Sloane, owner of the local knitting mills. Sloane built this house in 1895. After he moved to Norfolk, his home in South Norfolk was sold to George Washington Forehand. Dr. L.C. Ferebee's office was at 1222 Chesapeake Avenue. A house contractor, Fred Sherman lived at 1238, the large house on the corner of Chesapeake Avenue and Jefferson Street. William Sykes, a real estate agent, lived at 1416 Chesapeake Avenue. Dr. I.L. Chapman lived at 1446, which is at the corner of Chesapeake Avenue and Holly Street, and his office was in the basement. Steve Hollowell was Dr. Chapman's full-time driver. After Dr. Chapman, Drs. Bocock, Myers, and Jennings used the office. Dr. Jennings still practices medicine at this location. James A. Stephenson, who ran an insurance business, owned the home at 1500.

In 1910, members of one of the oldest families in Norfolk County, the Portlocks, moved into South Norfolk. The Portlocks are descended from early settlers and gave their name to the community of Portlock. Frank Livingston Portlock Sr. and his wife, Marion Hunter (West) Portlock, acquired the home that had belonged to William M. Tilley at 1007 Ohio Street. The Portlocks had three children: Marion, who was born in 1900; Eugenia, in 1906; and Frank L. Portlock Jr., who was born July 18, 1908. Frank Jr., who is 93 years of age, is the last of the Portlocks.

One of the most impressive houses in South Norfolk is the large Queen Anne–style house at 1146 Rodgers Street. Built in 1903 in a combination of cement block, brick, and wood, this was the home of the John Cuthrell family. It has been said that John mixed the cement himself and built the house to the second floor level before enlisting the help of an architect and contractor to finish the job. He lived in the house with his wife, Sarah, his children, a boarder, and one female servant, Mary Elizabeth Addington. Cuthrell owned an ice plant at the end of B Street across the Belt Line Railroad—this location later became the Grower's Exchange. In 1910, John owned a feed store, and by 1926, he was president of the Bank of South Norfolk. In 1939, Francis Gay bought the house from Cuthrell and turned it into a funeral home.

By the second decade of the twentieth century, South Norfolk had churches, a school, and stores, and a large number of residents owned their homes and either had businesses or were employed by nearby companies. South Norfolk was a flourishing unincorporated community in Washington Magisterial District, Norfolk County, and although a city in size and importance, it was without public improvements. There were no smooth surface streets, no sanitary sewerage and storm disposal system, or health facilities. Just prior to the close of World War I, certain citizens of the village held a meeting and it was decided that county government was not advantageous to a large and growing community like South Norfolk. By August 1919, it was obvious that Norfolk had intentions to annex South Norfolk. Most citizens of South Norfolk thought that annexation by Norfolk would result in lower taxes and better services for the community. On August 19, 1919, a meeting of the citizens of South Norfolk was called to discuss the subject of annexation and the issue of applying for a town charter. As a result of this meeting, strong opposition to annexation arose. Q.C. Davis Jr., a member of the Virginia General Assembly, was most instrumental in the change of position. Davis, with the assistance of State Senator Corbitt and the backing of Thomas Black and E.E. Meginley, prepared a bill for the Virginia Legislature, and in a rapid succession of events, a bill to incorporate the Town of South Norfolk was legislated. It became law on September 11, 1919, and South Norfolk began to function as a town on September 19, 1919. Q.C. Davis Jr. was the first mayor and E.L. Harper was appointed president of the nine-member council. The town had assets of more than $4 million.

Some ordinances approved by the town council in 1919 included the following: for shouting in streets or alleys, a fine of $5; for fast and dangerous driving of gasoline-driven or horse-drawn vehicles (15 miles per hour on streets, 10 miles per hour on corners), $15; for drunkenness or disorder, $1 to $25; for gambling or betting, $1 or 60 days in jail.

By December 22, 1920, the population of South Norfolk was 7,691, and Mayor Davis prepared a petition for the town to become a city of the second class. On January 5, 1921, South Norfolk, pursuant to law, became a city of the second class, with F.L. Rowland as mayor; Q.C. Davis Jr., first city attorney; W.T. Madrin, clerk; P.M. Warden, city sergeant; S.H. Dennis, treasurer; and E.H. Brown, commissioner of revenue.

At that time, South Norfolk comprised the territory bounded on the north by Berkley Avenue, on the east and south by the Virginian Railroad, and on the west by the Southern Branch of the Elizabeth River and Berkley.

The growth of South Norfolk was rapid. Numerous ornamental and attractive homes had been built on Chesapeake Avenue, which was to become the elite section of the community. Eventually, beautiful tall trees lined both sides of the

In 1917, the South Norfolk High School was made up of this small group of young adults. They are posing on the steps of their new building, which had been built the year before on the corner of B and Twentieth Streets.

street. Their branches formed an archway producing shade from spring until early fall of each year.

New construction continued throughout the 1920s and 1930s. The decade of the 1920s was a period of national prosperity. C.M. Jordan, W.P. Jordan, and associates financed construction of the Norfolk-Portsmouth (Jordan) Bridge. Permission to build the bridge was secured from the 69th Congress (Public Bill No. 272) on May 22, 1926. Messrs. Harrington, Howard & Ash, engineers from a firm in Kansas City, Missouri, designed the bridge, and E.R. Needles, of their New York office, oversaw construction. The contract was awarded on June 25, 1927, and work started August 15, 1927. The cost was $1,125,00, and the bridge was opened for traffic on August 24, 1928 in a dedication ceremony led by Governor Harry Flood Byrd.

By 1928, many new stores were beginning to appear on Poindexter and Liberty Streets, providing a larger shopping district.

The early streets were of dirt, rocks, or oyster shells, and sometimes a combination of these. When it rained, the streets were mostly mud. The sidewalks were boards fastened together to form boardwalks. Liberty Street had boardwalks on one side of the street that extended from the Norfolk & Western Railroad to the Belt Line Railroad near the Berkley line. A bond issue was floated in 1922 enabling the City to run sewer lines down the center of the principal streets, and 12 miles of lines were laid. A two-lane concrete strip was paved down most of the streets. Curbs and gutters were added in 1937 under a Works Progress Administration (WPA) project.

The new South Norfolk High School was built in 1929 at a cost of $140,430. In 1934, Cascade Park, one of the largest athletic fields in the vicinity of Norfolk, was built by the City at a cost of $5,000. The same year, the beautiful Lakeside Park was built with WPA funds at a cost of nearly $140,000.

Before the turn of the century, the area that became Lakeside Park was marshy and an inlet from the Southern Branch of the Elizabeth River reached that far. In the early 1900s, part of it was cleared and a large roof-covered dance pavilion was built (probably in the area where Byrd Avenue is today). The pavilion was approximately 200 feet by 100 feet. There were bleachers on either side and a centered bandstand, where bands played and dances were held several nights a week. The Berkley Street Railway and Light Company promoted this spot, and the company ran trolley cars from Chestnut Street in Berkley to Holly Street in South Norfolk. To encourage use of the trolley, they donated funds for installation of electric lights around the area. Most of the activities took place at night. A favorite activity was the cakewalk, which was a musical promenade where the prize of a cake was awarded to the couple who demonstrated the most imaginative or intricate dance steps. A narrow footbridge crossed the marsh to the pavilion. In the next few years, a merry-go-round and several concessions were added. There were also slides and barbecue pits. The local residents, visitors from Berkley, and workers from the nearby Elizabeth Knitting Mill used the facility.

For the next 30 years, nothing was done towards upkeep and the dance pavilion, merry-go-round, and other structures fell into disuse and decay. In the spring of

Federal funds were used in 1933 to turn marshland near Quincy Place into Lakeside Park.

1933, city attorney Q.C. Davis Jr., went to Washington as chairman of a committee formed to acquire funds for construction of Lakeside Park. He was successful and work started in the summer, with J.H. Massey as the consulting engineer. The work was done by hand, and many previously unemployed men were put to work. The lake was dug with shovels, and the dirt was carried away in wheelbarrows. Because the community had used the area for drainage, pumps were required to keep the water out. Gravel walks were laid and a rustic bridge was built out of lumber donated by Carl Jordan of Jordan Lumber Company. Greenbrier Farms planted trees and shrubs. Most of the trees were pines, which have since been replaced with oaks and magnolias. Plaques were placed in the ground at the base of each tree to commemorate those from South Norfolk who had died in World War I. Needless to say, all of the plaques disappeared over the years. Some were thrown into the lake and others just walked off into the sunset.

A spillway on the edge of the lake near Bainbridge Boulevard was constructed to keep the water level of the lake constant. A circular structure was built in the center of the lake. The plan was to install a water fountain, but the pipes were not connected. The lake was stocked with fish. The project was completed in the spring of 1934, and on June 16, 1934, the park was dedicated by Governor George Campbell Peery. A shovel that was used to plant the first dogwood tree in the park was inscribed by the governor, "To my friend, Q.C. Davis."

Over the years, many notable events have taken place in the park. One in particular is the sport of ice-skating. Even when the marsh was there, the water would freeze solid and people would come from miles around to skate, especially during the severe winter of 1918. During the author's youth, the lake froze almost every winter.

In March 1995, the City of Chesapeake spent approximately $1 million on a major renovation of Lakeside Park. It is still a place of beauty where band concerts, summer church services, art shows, picnics, family reunions, and other events take place. One of the most popular gatherings is the family day in the park, which is held every July 4.

Another place that provided recreation in the early years of the twentieth century was Johnson's pond. Information received from early residents of South Norfolk indicates that there were actually two ponds, one was referred to as the big pond and the other the small pond. The big pond ran from Stewart Street across that section where Bainbridge Boulevard is today, near the Belt Line Railroad, and continued on where the city dump was located in later years. The structure that served as Overton's warehouse was built on land that had been the edge of the pond. Part of the pond was filled and Hutchinson's Market was located on it. A small section still remains in the 200 block of D Street. There was a large drainage ditch, which began approximately 100 yards from Poindexter Street between what is now the 1000 block of Stewart Street and Bainbridge Boulevard. This ditch, the edges of which were covered with willow trees, ran down to and emptied into the big pond. This body of fresh water would freeze in winter and many residents gathered there to ice skate or watch others skate.

The small pond was on the opposite side of the Belt Line Railroad near Berkley and ran down to the Elizabeth River. There was a dam, which controlled the flow of water and prevented the pond from emptying. This was a salt-water pond, which was used by the Greenleaf Johnson Lumber Company. Logs that had been floated down the river were pulled through a gorge to the pond, where they were stored until the company was ready to process them.

The area south of the large pond was known as Johnson's woods and was at one time a part of the Tunis, Johnson farm. Prior to World War II, Bainbridge Boulevard came to an end at Poindexter Street and that area between Poindexter and Grady Streets was woodland. There were several houses on the other side of the woods on what was known as Bainbridge extended. In the early 1940s, a group of 400 apartments were built off Bainbridge extended, the woods were removed, and Bainbridge Boulevard was continued on to Berkley. The apartments backed up to the Elizabeth River in the vicinity across from the Navy Yard, where Admiral Poindexter had built his first home. It was determined that an appropriate name for the apartment complex would be Admiral's Road. The original Admiral's Road began at the Poindexter home (the Anchorage) on the waterfront, meandered through the areas that became South Norfolk and Portlock, and came to an end at the old Providence Church at the corner of Great and Chair Roads. Today, Great Road is Campostella Road, and Chair Road is Providence Road.

A familiar sight along the Southern Branch of the Elizabeth River was that of the steamboat *Emma Kay*. The *Emma Kay*, whose skipper was Captain Snow, brought produce from the farms of North Carolina to the Roanoke docks in Norfolk. It made several stops along the way and picked up passengers. One regular passenger was Margaret West, a student at Deep Creek High School. She rode the boat to and from school each day. After completing her education, Miss West taught English and history at South Norfolk and Oscar Smith High Schools for almost 50 years.

The schedule of the *Emma Kay* was well known to the boys of South Norfolk and Berkley. For in the summer months, most of them swam nude in the Elizabeth River. When the boat appeared around the bend, they all ran for cover until it passed.

Before the end of the nineteenth century and up until the South Norfolk High School was built on Holly Street, the section was mostly woods and marshland. Eventually, part of the land was cleared and became a ball field for the local boys and another part was used by the neighbors for gardens. This tract of land was part of the Portlock estate and stretched from Holly Street to the Virginian Railroad. Other property owners in the area were Irvin Truitt, John Etheridge, Rosa Etheridge, and Mrs. Indy Seymore. The tract across the Virginian Railroad and down by the creek was the John Massenburg property. The Portlocks owned another strip of land, which was dug out, and the dirt was sold for construction of the overpass over the Virginian Railroad on Bainbridge Boulevard. Some of the dirt was also used in construction of an overpass on Campostella Road near where the Carver School is located. Henry Clay Hofheimer was awarded the contract to build the overpass on Bainbridge Boulevard. It was built at a cost of $197,000 and was dedicated in 1937.

The creek that was near the Massenburg property and is now next to the Southgate Plaza Shopping Center is a part of Jones Creek. All the low land along Rodgers Street across from the Oscar Smith Stadium was part of "Big Hill" and the Massenburg property. The Massenburg cemetery was located in front of what is now the main entrance to the stadium. The land between the stadium and the Oscar Smith School was at one time the city dump.

In the 1930s, there was a popular story about the town drunk. It seems that every Saturday night he would tie one on, and so, some of his fellow drinkers decided to play a joke on him. One Saturday night after he passed out, they carried him to the Massenburg cemetery. Well, there was this sunken grave, where they very carefully placed him and tucked him in for the night. When the sun came up Sunday morning and he awoke, his first thought was that he had died. It has been said that after this he never touched another drop and acquired some new friends.

In 1927, Irvin Truitt of Truitt-Smith Reality Corporation began development of a new residential section on part of the land that he had acquired from the heirs of William Nathaniel Portlock. This new development would be given the name "Avalon." It was advertised as the ideal location for a real home and only minutes from any action of the city. There were no utility poles on the streets, for they

Bainbridge Boulevard residents enjoy a swim in the street on August 23, 1933 after a hurricane caused flooding from the Elizabeth River and Mill Dam Creek. This would not be the last time the intersection of Bainbridge and Freeman Avenues would be under water.

were all installed in the alley behind the houses. There was a building restriction of $5,000.

At the end of Virginia Avenue were the Briquette Plant and a tall steel tower that was used when unloading coal dust from the trains. The dust was mixed with oil and compressed into briquettes. When used in a stove or furnace, the briquettes produced a very hot fire.

After many years, the plant was closed and the surrounding land was developed with total disregard for the original survey, which had been done by Franklin L. Portlock Sr. Today, there are many streets winding in and out and quite a few cul-de-sacs. The rationale was that more houses could be built by changing from the previous survey.

Until recent years, there was a spur line that ran between the Norfolk & Western Railroad and the Virginian Railroad. In the early 1960s, the area between the spur line and Freeman Avenue became Varsity Manor. This had been part of the Tapley Portlock farm. The farmhouse, which still stands, was built c. 1789. After the Portlocks, the Gibsons owned the property and the surrounding area was known as Gibson Hill. Gibson Acres is that land between Freeman Avenue and Portlock Road. Elmer Gordon developed most of this area.

The Portlock farmhouse was located a short distance from the intersection of Portlock Road and Franklin Street near Bainbridge Boulevard. Portlock Road ran

Ms. Hassell and the family dog pose for a picture on the Bainbridge Boulevard streetcar tracks in 1930. Streetcars ran to Portlock until the overpass was built in 1937, when they were replaced by buses. The tall building to the left is J.M. Hyatt's confectionery and to its right is the local barbershop.

straight to the front gate of the farmhouse. In order to reach Bainbridge Boulevard, one had to detour down Freeman Avenue. There was a lane that was used by the Portlock family, which ran from the farm to Freeman Avenue. Portlock Station was on the corner of Freeman Avenue and Bainbridge Boulevard. This is where the streetcar stopped to pick up passengers.

Nathaniel Portlock (1814–1863) built his farmhouse in 1854. The tract of land, which covered 52 acres, was originally granted to the Portlock family by the king of England. The boundaries were Freeman Avenue, Franklin Street, and Mill Dam Creek. Nathaniel Portlock named the residence the "Oaks." Judge William Nathaniel Portlock, son of Franklin and Eugenia Herbert (Tatem) Portlock, referred to it as "the Home Place." William's brother Franklin L. Portlock Sr. and his family lived there and tended the farm until they moved to South Norfolk in 1910.

Uncle Virgil came from North Carolina and went to work for Franklin Portlock. He did various jobs around the farm, and when the family moved to South Norfolk, he went with them. Their house on Ohio Street had a large basement with ceilings that were 7 feet in height. It was there that Virgil made his home. He milked the cows, kept the lawn, shoveled snow in winter, and did other chores as needed.

After the family moved to South Norfolk, Portlock rented the farm to A.S. Jones. Its ownership remained in the family until 1939. On September 2, 1939, Robert Rowland purchased the property. The old farmhouse was relocated to the edge of Mill Dam Creek, which is now Hamilton Street. Rowland, along with Simeon Leary, developed the land and gave it the name "Portlock Terrace." There were two oak trees in the backyard of the farmhouse, and they are still standing today along Portlock Road.

After the post–Civil War depression, the industrial potential of South Norfolk began to be realized through two railroad lines, the Norfolk & Western and the Virginian. With its location so close to Norfolk, South Norfolk was a natural for suburban development. The railroad lines and proximity to the Elizabeth River also made it a natural for industry.

Early South Norfolk was like the hub of a wheel. The bulk of the industries were either in South Norfolk or the territory immediately surrounding it on both sides of the Southern Branch of the Elizabeth River. It was there that large amounts of manufactured goods were shipped out and raw materials shipped in. A large number of the fertilizer, chemical, guano, and oil companies were located in the Money Point section of Portlock.

It was about 1870 when Carter B. Poindexter and his son Parke brought the first manufacturing plant of importance in this section by inducing the firm of Johnson & Waters of Baltimore to locate here. This plant later became the Greenleaf Johnson Lumber Company. Other manufacturing mills soon located in the vicinity and drew a large number of people for employment.

One of the earliest industries was the processing of lumber. Logs were chained together and floated to the area by way of the intracoastal waterway from the

Carolinas and southern parts of Virginia. Among the early lumber mills along the waterfront were those of LeKies and Collins, E.M. Tilley (located at Montalant), Tunis and Serpell, Arbuckle, and Greenleaf Johnson. Tunis and Serpell became the Tunis Lumber Company. Theophilus Tunis was president, and he also served as a state senator.

Another major industry was the creosoting of piles, lumber, ties, posts, and other wood products. Creosote is made by the distillation of coal and wood tar and is used as a coating to preserve wood. Wood treated with creosote can spend many years in the ground without rotting. There were several creosoting works at Money Point on the Southern Branch. Among them were the Old Dominion Creosoting Plant, Norfolk, Republic, Eppington-Russell, Wycoff, and Atlantic creosoting companies. These plants contributed heavily to the pollution of the Elizabeth River over the years, but the U.S. Army Corps of Engineers is currently testing a site between Scuffletown Creek and the Jordan Bridge for cleanup.

Industries continued to expand, as did the shipments of coal over the Norfolk & Western and Virginian Railroads. By 1910, in addition to F.S. Royster Company, there was the Pocomont Guano Company and the Swift and Company Fertilizer Plant. There were two major oil companies, the Mexican Petroleum Company and the Texas Oil Company, both of which operated large distribution plants. There were also six mills that manufactured lumber, boxes, laths, shingles, hardwood, mahogany, and other millwork.

The James G. Wilson Corporation made steel blinds and rolling and sliding doors of all kinds, many of which were exported. The company employed approximately 500 men and worked an average of eight and three-quarter hours per day and five and a half days per week. The company also produced partitions, which were used in the largest buildings in the world.

The firm of A.S. Lee & Sons Company, Inc., manufacturers of agricultural lime and fertilizer, had its factory on Barnes Road. Arthur S. Lee of Richmond had established it, but in December 1933, Walter B. Mann and his associates acquired the business. It then became the Reliance Fertilizer and Lime Corporation. After Walter Mann's death in March 1947, James Justin Joyce became president, and Mrs. Marguerite Joyce Mann of South Norfolk, vice president.

By 1926, there were three factories manufacturing lime and fertilizer, and they supplied the farms in the vicinity of South Norfolk and Norfolk County. A new cement plant had just been completed, and it had a capacity of 3,600 barrels per day. The plant employed 180 day laborers besides the salaried men. It had a payroll of $1,250 each week, which did not include the monthly salaried employees (the laboratory and clerical force of about ten men). The Norfolk & Southern Railroad shops and the other local railroad facilities also helped to provide an economical base for the community.

The Elizabeth Knitting Mill was on Perry Street in South Norfolk, where the Rena B. Wright School is now. The Chesapeake Knitting Mill was near the Berkley–South Norfolk line and employed a large number of South Norfolk residents. Most of the employees were paid by the piece (piecework).

In 1902, J.H. Norton, who lived on Chesapeake Avenue, opened the Shirtwaist Factory on Poindexter Street. The factory was charted by the county court in July 1902. On July 30, 1902, the *Virginian-Pilot* newspaper announced that the factory was ready to start operation in 10 days and would employ about 100 people. Sometime later, Norton moved the factory to Thirteenth and Liberty Streets, and a Mr. Hoffner, who owned the building, turned the former factory into apartments. The Hoffner apartments were demolished around 1951.

The E.H. Barnes Company opened and produced box shooks and lumber. They also purchased logs for processing. Consumer's Box Company, at the corner of Seaboard Avenue and Guerrier Street, manufactured barrels, wooden strawberry crates, and other types of wooden containers. John Loeffeet was the proprietor. One of the office employees was Uncle John Gaydell, who was known for the large murals that he painted on the walls of the Grand Theatre.

Other plants of importance included the Lone Star Cement Company, N. Block and Sons-Salvage, Interstate Sand Company, Riley Tar Company, and Eastern Tar Products. All these plants represented an investment of several million dollars and they paid thousands of dollars in taxes to the community. They also furnished employment for a large number of citizens of South Norfolk and the surrounding areas.

South Norfolk advertised the availability of industrial sites, three trunk line railroads, and also the Norfolk and Portsmouth Belt Line Railroad, which handled trade to and from all points without additional cost to the shipper or consignee. The City publicized an ample water supply, cheap electric power, and deep water on the Southern Branch. South Norfolk cooperated with prospective industries to see that their requirements were supplied in a satisfactory manner. An example was the reinforcement of a concrete road at a cost of $3,400, which led to the Virginia Portland Cement Corporation Plant.

In an early twentieth-century edition of the *Virginian-Pilot* newspaper, South Norfolk boasted of a population of 1,500 that was served by three railroads, two box factories, four sawmills, one chemical works, three guano plants, two churches, two public schools, a post office, and its own waterworks. The article ended with a promotional blurb stating that "With our good schools, smooth streets, nice sidewalks, plenty of churches, pure water, employment for all and money to let, we can say that those desiring a good investment could do no better than to cast their lot here. . . . we are looking for good citizens and no others need apply." Sounds like they were looking for a few good men.

It was in 1796 that Thomas Jefferson introduced his plan for the "General Diffusion of Knowledge" for Virginia. Through his influence and suggestion, on December 22, 1796, the General Assembly of Virginia enacted a school law, entitled "An Act to Establish Schools." Two years later, Norfolk County adopted Jefferson's plan and put into operation a system of public education.

The future president described the type of educational program that he thought was needed by the Commonwealth when he wrote, "A system of education which shall reach every description of citizens from the richest to the poorest, as it was the earliest, so will it be the latest of all public concerns in which I shall permit myself to take interest." The county's leaders accepted this point of view, and it has served as a guide during ensuing years, both for citizens of Norfolk County and for that area of the county that in 1919 became the town of South Norfolk.

For a number of years, the children from McCloudtown (as South Norfolk was then known) and nearby farms attended the schools of Berkley. After the Civil War, during the Reconstruction period, the people who could afford to do so employed tutors for their children. Around 1872, the Providence School was established at the intersection of what is today Campostella and Providence Roads. The next public school was at Money Point. Classes were held in a church until a school in the village of Portlock was completed around 1895. This school was a one-room frame building.

The history of Rosemont Christian Church relates to using the school for holding prayer meetings in 1902. When the one-room structure was completed, Miss Rena B. Wright, the teacher at Money Point, moved with her students to the school in Portlock. Miss Wright taught at this school for two or three years. For a while, the school at Portlock continued to be known as the Money Point School.

On August 31, 1895, School District Number Five of Norfolk County acquired a parcel of land in Washington Magisterial District from the Shea family. The land was situated on the east side of the public road, which had been formerly known as the Berkley and Currituck Turnpike. The road was 40 feet wide. It is interesting to note the descriptive location of the stakes placed by the surveyors—one being in the branch near a spring on the roadside, another in the center of a cove—and the reference made to the lines of the lands of B.F. Gibson and A.A. Spain. The deed stated that the piece of land "contained an acre, less a fraction of an acre" and that the school district would have the right to use the spring on the roadside located near the northwest corner of the land. This property, on which a new four-room brick school was eventually built, was purchased for the sum of $150.

The first school to be established in the village of South Norfolk was a private school. Around 1890, the Elizabeth Knitting Mill was operating on Park Avenue between Perry and Porter Streets. At that time, there were no labor laws and a number of children were employed at the mill. They usually worked six days a week. When the depression occurred in 1893, the mill cut back to three days a week—Thursday, Friday, and Saturday. This meant that there were three days that the children could not work. The parents collectively asked Mrs. Edward Williams if she would teach them. Mrs. Williams had been teaching her own children, so she consented to teach the others as well. For two years she used the second floor of her home for this purpose. During this time, she had about 15 pupils and received $1 per month for each student. The Williams homestead was located near Scuffletown Creek at what later became known as 1710 Porter Street. The locals referred to Scuffletown as Scufflintown. According to tradition, the name came from the sound made by dancers at the dances that were regularly held in the village.

A public school was organized in South Norfolk as early as August 1891. Forming an organization called the "South Norfolk School Society," a group of men of the community erected a two-room wooden school building on property acquired from E.M. Tilley. The school was built on Jackson Street in what is now the 1100 block between Guerriere and Ohio Streets. The cost of the school, including the furniture and outbuilding, was approximately $2,200. The teachers were Miss Annie Gammon and Miss Lucy Scott. (Miss Scott later became Mrs. H.W. Keeling.) Captain John T. West was superintendent of Norfolk County schools at that time.

The enrollment continued to increase and a third room was added. The faculty then consisted of Miss Grace Coggins (principal), Miss Blanche Hines Barrie, and Miss Frances Wray. When Miss Coggins married, Miss Rena B. Wright took her place. There was a rule that married teachers, except under extenuating circumstances, would not be employed by the school. This rule was followed until there was a severe shortage of teachers during World War II. In 1946, after the war ended, married teachers were no longer placed under contract, and each received a letter from the superintendent of schools thanking them for their service during the emergency. It also stated that they would not be rehired.

When Miss Wright came to South Norfolk, she expected to stay only two months, but remained in the school system until she retired in June 1942. After retiring, she lived with her sister in Norfolk. Miss Rena B. Wright died on March 16, 1946.

Just prior to 1900, enrollment at the Jackson Street School had increased to the point where some classes were held in the Odd Fellows Hall on Poindexter Street.

Miss Virginia Hicks, driver training teacher for South Norfolk High School, accepts a dual-control car loaned by the Peebles Motor Co. in January 1947.

To participate in the annual Five Pointers' parade, children had to pass minimum requirements for physical fitness in five categories: weight, hearing, teeth, throat, and vision. In 1955, these healthy second-graders filed past a Texaco station. The large building to the left had been a Ford dealership and later the city garage.

The small wooden building on Jackson Street was soon inadequate for the growing community, and the school board of Washington District purchased a block of land in Elmsley. The block was bounded by A, B, Twentieth, and Twenty-second Streets. The first brick building of eight rooms was built around 1902 at a cost of $35,000. There were five teachers in the new building, including the principal, Miss Rena B. Wright.

In 1906, plans were made to form a high school, though there were only three teachers certified to teach the higher grades. This high school was among the first, if not the first, in Norfolk County. During this period pupils desiring work in the sixth grade or higher came to South Norfolk from Portlock, Campostella, and from as far away as Oak Grove. Students from Portlock and Money Point rode the streetcar, and their fare was paid by the school board. Pupils from Campostella, which was a part of Norfolk, walked, and those from Oak Grove came on a mule-drawn wagon driven by Lewis Curling Sr.

In 1908, John W. Jones built a four-room brick school in Portlock. This building has undergone a renovation recently and reopened in May 1997 as the Chesapeake's Museum and Information Center. Two other schools were constructed in 1908. One of them, the South Hill Elementary School, was built at the corner of Hill Street and Hanna Avenue and served about 300 students. The other, named for George Washington Carver, was built off Campostella Road.

Between 1906 and 1908, more students were advancing toward the high school level. Around 1909, construction of a second building was begun in Elmsley on B

Street, and a large hall connected the two eight-room structures. This new building was ready to accept students in September 1910 and was used as the high school. Just two years later, more classrooms were needed, and the old school on Jackson Street was moved to the grounds on B Street. This building had no running water, so the larger boys were detailed to carry buckets of water to the classes in the morning and again in the afternoon. Outhouses were erected behind this temporary building. A third brick building was constructed at the corner of B and Twentieth Streets and was occupied in 1916. At that time, the old wooden structure from Jackson Street was torn down.

In 1914, the Waterford School on Liberty Street was built. It received an addition in 1959. The school and grounds covered 1.3 acres and had a capacity of 510 students. A three-story brick high school was built in the village of Portlock in 1922. Several other high schools were erected in Norfolk County that year, and they were all built using the same plans.

Once again the school on B Street became overcrowded and a 6-acre site was purchased on Holly Street. The new South Norfolk High School was built in 1929, and the first students entered the new school on February 3, 1930.

The Great Depression hit in 1929, and several WPA projects mentioned previously helped ease the economic pain for a limited number of people. Many students had to quit school and seek employment to help their families make ends meet. Hard times continued throughout the country until the United States was forced to enter World War II. The war touched the lives of every family in more ways than one. Those in a certain age bracket answered our county's call, and all remember the draft board on A Street.

With the onset of the war and the many shortages that accompanied it, rationing became a way of life. In May 1942, the Office of Price Administration (OPA) opened local board number 65-4 at 701 St. James Street, where rationing books were issued to the families of South Norfolk. Before the war ended in 1945, gasoline, tires, fuel oil, shoes, meats, sugar, and most other food items were rationed. When the war ended, many of those who had not finished high school used the G.I. Bill and returned to the classroom.

In 1947, the newly formed Junior Chamber of Commerce petitioned the City to change the form of government from the mayor-council to the city manager form. A referendum was held on April 1, 1947, and the vote was 669 for and 501 against. The new form of government went into effect on September 1, 1947. The position of city manager was very transitory; most did not last more than two years.

On March 18, 1948, the village of Portlock was chartered as a town. Governor William Tuck appointed Simeon S. Leary as interim mayor until a regular election could be held on the second Tuesday of June. Leary served until June 8 of that year, and then H.S. Boyette became mayor.

In October 1949, South Norfolk won its bid for annexation of the Town of Portlock. At that time, the court suggested July 1, 1950, as the effective date of the decree. The *Norfolk-Virginian Pilot* of October 14, 1949, stated that as a result of the annexation South Norfolk would triple in size and double in population. Prior to this, South Norfolk covered an area approximately 5 miles by 7 miles. With the annexation, the area increased by 224 percent, and the population reached 20,896. In order to become a city of the first class, South Norfolk needed a population of 10,000. This requirement had been met, and shortly thereafter, South Norfolk became a city of the first class.

Continued increase in school enrollment called for other schools to be built. Early in 1950, the City of South Norfolk purchased 26 acres at the foot of Rodgers Street. It was there that the first Oscar F. Smith High School was built at a cost of about $1 million. Students occupied the school in September 1954. Forty years later, this became a middle school and a new Oscar F. Smith High School opened on Great Bridge Boulevard.

After the merger, other schools were built in the South Norfolk area. A new elementary school was erected on a 23-acre site at 1857 Varsity Drive in 1964, and later, another elementary school was constructed on the property where the Elizabeth Knitting Mill was once located. This school was named in memory of Rena B. Wright, the longtime teacher, and was dedicated on October 24, 1971. The first school in Riverdale Manor was built in 1943 and was known as the Riverdale Elementary School. This later became Park Elementary and then the Thurgood Marshall Elementary School at 2706 Border Road.

Early churches served not only as places of worship but also hosted such events as school graduations, picnics, and many other happenings of the day. The Providence Christian Church was one of the early churches of Norfolk County. Elder N.P. Tatem organized the church in 1804 with the assistance of a group of

When this picture of A Street was taken in 1957, most of the buildings' occupants were long gone. One tenant the citizens were happy to see go was the South Norfolk office of the draft board.

ministers. The church was situated 4 miles from Norfolk on the highway to Great Bridge. The land on which it was built was purchased with English pounds. Available information places the house of worship at the corner of Providence and Campostella Roads. It was a part of St. Brides Parish, which had been formed from the Elizabeth River Parish in 1761.

The first church in South Norfolk was the Liberty Street Methodist Episcopal Church, South, which was dedicated in May 1892. After moving to Chesapeake Avenue, the name was changed to reflect its new location. The South Norfolk Baptist Church followed the Methodist Church. The building opened for worship on January 5, 1893, and the formal dedication took place on June 11, 1893, at 3:30 in the afternoon.

Around 1900, the leading citizens of the village of Portlock became concerned about having a place of worship in the community. Most of them were attending the Providence Christian Church a few miles away. On August 14, 1902, Dr. J. Pressley Barrett, who was pastor of the Memorial Christian Temple in Norfolk, organized the Rosemont Christian Church. Most of the members of the Providence Church transferred their membership to either Rosemont or the Memorial Christian Temple at Thirty-third Street and Llewellyn Avenue in Norfolk.

In the fall of 1903, a Sunday school was organized in the old South Norfolk School on Jackson Street. From its beginning, the Sunday school had a steady growth, and on May 29, 1904, the South Norfolk Congregational Christian Church was organized.

The official beginning of the Raleigh Heights Baptist Church in Norfolk County was on November 10, 1897. It had originally been known as the Broadway Baptist Mission School. It is possible that the mission started as early as 1895 at the Dozier's Corner community when the men considered an alternative to the 3-mile horse-and-cart ride in inclement weather to the South Norfolk Baptist Church. A new road to Portlock was built around 1906 and land opened for development. A place to meet was needed and the Portlock School was made available. On December 29, 1916, a deed was recorded conveying property from the Raleigh Heights Development Corporation to the trustees of the Broadway Church. A building was completed and dedicated in 1918.

The South Norfolk Church of Christ had its beginning in 1906. In 1910, the building on the corner of Chesapeake Avenue and Poindexter Street was constructed in just six days under the leadership of John W. Tyndall, president of the Industrial Christian College of Kinston, North Carolina. The church split, and as a result, there are now two churches, the Laurel Avenue Church of Christ at 1126 Laurel Avenue and the South Norfolk Church of Christ at 2526 Rodgers Street.

The South Norfolk Pentecostal Holiness Church was organized in October 1912 with 26 charter members. A tent was used near the corner of Liberty and Commerce Streets, and Reverend F.W. Gammon became the first pastor. The congregation later met in an old fish house and then an abandoned grocery store.

In May 1913, they began meeting in a frame tabernacle. In 1933, the tabernacle was replaced with a structure built on land at the corner of Liberty and Commerce Streets. Expansions were made in 1947 and 1949. In 1956, the building received brick veneer.

In March 1919, the First Presbyterian Church of South Norfolk had its beginning as a Sunday school. The original name of the church was the Geneva Presbyterian Church, and it was organized on November 1, 1920. The church records do not state when the name was changed to the First Presbyterian Church of South Norfolk, but it appears that it might have taken place around 1940.

In 1923, under the ministry of W. Farley Powers, the Portlock Methodist Church began in the old four-room school building, which is now the home of Chesapeake's Museum. The first church building was built on Edgewood Avenue. The first service there was held on Sunday, May 3, 1925. In 1968, ground was broken for a sanctuary and educational building on Bainbridge Boulevard.

The South Norfolk Assembly of God was born out of a tent meeting, which was held by Mrs. Myrtle Chambers in July 1926. Chambers was an evangelist and she held meetings in the tent on the northeast corner of Bainbridge Boulevard. The next place of worship used was a tin building on Bainbridge Boulevard, which had been an automobile repair shop. On Sunday, March 29, 1931, the congregation of 164 members met at the building on Bainbridge Boulevard, where Reverend J.M. Oliver led them in prayer, and they marched to their new church that had been built on Decatur Street.

The Southside Baptist Church began as a Sunday school under the direction of the South Norfolk Baptist Church. The church, located on Perry Street, was organized in March 1952 as the Southside Baptist Church with 64 charter members.

Numerous branches and creeks emptied into the Elizabeth River, and these streams, along with the river itself, divided Norfolk County into three sections, making public ferries necessary for the convenience of the people from the time of the earliest settlement.

The first steam ferry, the *Gosport*, was built in Portsmouth and outfitted with engines in Philadelphia. It made its first trip across the harbor between Norfolk and Portsmouth in 1832. The approximate time was 5 minutes. Another early steam ferry was the *Union*, so named because it served as a link between the twin cities by the sea. Captain William Chiles was its engineer.

From 1862 to 1865, Federal forces operated the ferries. At the turn of the century, the ferry rates were as follows: for foot passengers, a single ticket was 3¢ and two or more tickets were 2.5¢ each; for man and horse, a single ticket was 8¢ and two or more tickets were 7.5¢ each; for bicycle and rider, all tickets were 5¢. There were several sidewheel ferryboats, the *Rockaway*, the *City of Norfolk*, and the *City of Portsmouth*. These ferryboats ran from Berkley to Portsmouth or to Commercial Place in downtown Norfolk.

The first horse-driven streetcars officially began operation in Norfolk on August 12, 1870. Around 1873, James McNeal attempted to establish passenger service between McCloud's Store and Berkley. The establishment of J. Alonza

The South Norfolk Congregational Christian Church is seen here on July 21, 1926. First organized as a Sunday school in 1903, the church grew to 16 members by the following year.

McCloud and son was located on Liberty Street in South Norfolk. McNeal's venture failed for lack of passengers. The area was very sparsely populated and his service was a little premature. The small horse-driven streetcar that began serving Berkley in 1888 was extended to the intersection of Chesapeake Avenue and Guerriere Street in South Norfolk. In 1893, the Berkley Street Railway Company consisted of 20 head of horses and mules and 7 cars. The stables were located behind the Baptist Church in South Norfolk. The cars, which were used on the run between South Norfolk and the Berkley Ferry, could be identified by the large sign near the top, which read "SO NORFOLK PARK'S & FERRIES." In 1894, the streetcars were electrified, enabling them to be propelled by means of a trolley and overhead wire. By this time, the run had been extended to the park on Holly Street in South Norfolk and then on to the village of Portlock and to the industrialized area of Money Point.

In 1937, an overpass was constructed over the Virginian Railroad and the streetcars to Portlock were replaced with buses. The streetcar line ended at Lakeside Park on Holly Street.

In May 1952, a new $23 million Norfolk-Portsmouth tunnel and Berkley Bridge complex was opened to traffic. The last streetcar was ceremoniously driven out of South Norfolk by Mayor Clarence Forehand. The tracks were either removed or in some cases were just covered over by asphalt. Eventually, the old Berkley Bridge at the end of South Main Street in Berkley was removed.

In February 1953, South Norfolk received its own corporation court, and Q.C. Davis Jr. became the first judge. After Judge Davis passed away on August 31, 1954, Jerry G. Bray became judge of the South Norfolk Corporation Court. Justice Herman White continued to run the civil and police court. Edwin Jones served as the clerk of the civil and police court from January 20, 1953, to October 1, 1955. In the latter part of 1953, construction of a new corporation court building was begun between the municipal building and the combination fire and police building.

During its municipality, South Norfolk had had eight mayors, beginning with Q.C. Davis Jr., when it became a town in 1919. When the town became a city of the second class in 1921, Floyd L. Rowland defeated Thomas Black in the run for mayor. Benjamin Harrison Gibson succeeded Mayor Rowland. In June 1929, S. Herman Dennis Sr. defeated Mayor Gibson in his bid for reelection but died eight days later. Judge Charles W. Coleman of the Circuit Court of Norfolk County appointed Gibson to continue as mayor. In 1936, Mayor Gibson died and J. James Davis was appointed to fill his unexpired term. Mayor Davis later ran against his cousin Q.C. Davis Jr., was reelected, and served until 1947. Clarence Forehand was elected to the city council in 1947 and was elected by his fellow councilmen to serve as mayor. He was the first mayor under the new city manager form of government. In 1953, N.J. Babb became the seventh mayor of South Norfolk. Linwood L. Briggs Jr. became mayor in 1957 and served until September 1961. Charles Richardson succeeded Briggs, and became the last mayor of the City of South Norfolk.

Marion White Nichols, Lil Hart, and Julian Raper check the construction of the South Norfolk Corporation Court building on November 30, 1953. An unidentified man stands to the right. Hart is now clerk of the Circuit Court of the City of Chesapeake.

Four of the five members of council were from the area that had been annexed by the City of South Norfolk. Before the end of the year, meetings were being held with Norfolk County politicians and merger was discussed. Norfolk County's losses in area, population, and revenue began in 1872 when the City of Norfolk began a series of 23 annexations, beginning with Atlantic City and ending with Tanners Creek in 1955. Portsmouth and South Norfolk annexed other areas. By December 22, 1961, a consolidation agreement for the City of South Norfolk and Norfolk County had been drawn up. This agreement covered all aspects of the merger. It also stated that the new city would consist of South Norfolk and the five magisterial districts of Norfolk County and that these would be South Norfolk, Butts Road, Deep Creek, Pleasant Grove, Washington, and Western Branch.

The *Virginia-Carolina News* of Thursday, January 25, 1962, reported on a merger meeting that was held at the B.M. Williams School. The panel of representatives consisted of Charles B. Cross, clerk of the court of Norfolk County; R.H. Waldo, commissioner of the revenue; J.A. Hodges, sheriff of Norfolk County; A.O. Lynch, treasurer; Peter M. Axson, commonwealth attorney; and Eugene Wadesworth, supervisor of Washington District. Their primary concern was the loss of Norfolk County citizens and taxes due to annexation. From 1948 to 1962, the county had lost 33 square miles by annexation.

South Norfolk Corporation Court Judge Jerry G. Bray Jr. and Norfolk County Circuit Court Judge Major M. Hillard set the date for the merger referendum, which was held on Tuesday, February 13, 1962. The consolidation was approved by a vote of 6,648 to 3,432. The next step was to be granted a charter by the General Assembly of Virginia.

After receiving approval from the General Assembly, it was decided that a name for the new city would be chosen in a later referendum. A total of 12 names appeared on the ballot:

Bridgeport	Great Bridge
Chesapeake	Norcova
Churchland	Port Elizabeth
Glendale	Sunray
Glennville	Virginia City
Gosport	Woodford

The name Chesapeake received 3,130 votes and the next highest was Great Bridge with 1,883 votes, so Chesapeake won. With all of this political maneuvering accomplished, the City of Chesapeake came into being on January 1, 1963.

6. Western Branch

The Chesapeake community of Western Branch is located between the Nansemond River and the Western Branch of the Elizabeth River. The Chesapeake and Nansemond Indians were the closest tribes to Western Branch. Dumpling Island on the Nansemond River, about 8 miles west of Western Branch, was home to a large village of Nansemond Indians of about 850 people. Dumpling Island was also an important trading post where the English came to trade with the Indians. The Chesapeake Indians occupied the land between the Elizabeth River and the ocean and were enemies to the Powhatan and Nansemond tribes. In fact, the Chesapeake Indians' culture and people were all but wiped out by wars with the other two tribes.

In 1632, when the General Assembly divided Virginia into eight shires or counties, Western Branch was a part of the Elizabeth City shire. The Elizabeth City shire became new Norfolk County in 1636 and was subsequently divided into Upper and Lower Norfolk County. In April 1691, Lower Norfolk County was split into two separate units, Norfolk and Princess Anne Counties. The community of Western Branch was a part of Norfolk County and remained so until the merger with the City of South Norfolk on January 1, 1963.

The farmers of Western Branch received their land in the early 1600s as a gift, a purchase, or a headright. A gift was when the King of England granted land to an individual as repayment for a favor or debt, while a headright was when the crown of England gave 50 acres to a colonist for each new member sponsored into the colony. There were many settlers in Western Branch, and the largest landowners were John Sipsey, who owned 1,500 acres; James Knoch, 1,200 acres; and Francis Hough, 800 acres.

The oldest house in Western Branch, built in 1690, can be found in Green Meadow Point East on Drum Creek. The Bruce-Speers house was erected in 1690 on a land grant to Charles William Bruce and Richard William Bruce, cousins of King Charles I of England. The house boasted a mill, a wharf, and a brick kiln. The wharf had the only deepwater landing on Drum Creek; therefore, the Churchpoint Plantation was able to ship goods to England, Norfolk, Baltimore, and New York. The house itself was built on an Indian burial site and is thought to be haunted by at least four or five ghosts. In 1720, a larger plantation house was constructed and the original house became the overseer's residence.

The years before the Revolutionary War with England were turbulent in Western Branch, as taxes and problems with England were felt on the farms and plantations. Patrick Henry's words "give me liberty or give me death" alarmed Governor Dunmore to the extent that he took the colonies' guns and gunpowder and hid them. Many men from Western Branch, worried about the safety of their families, enlisted in the Continental Army. Western Branch was ready for war and Norfolk County was asked to furnish 56 men. Those who helped England lost their land after the war and it was sold at auction. Many Loyalists returned to England.

The economy of Western Branch during this period was mainly agricultural, as early settlers found good soil for their crops. Tobacco was a main crop and was even accepted as legal currency. By 1705, when one sold a "hogshead" (barrel) of tobacco, the person received a "tobacco note," which became money in that county. The wages of Norfolk County officials, clergymen, and soldiers were paid with tobacco. The economy of Western Branch was also dependent upon the prosperous truck farms in the area. Before the introduction of the refrigerator car in the railroad system, the Western Branch area was situated in a key position to supply the vegetable needs of the great Northern cities. Following the Civil War, stops along the Norfolk & Southern Railroad at Centerville, Hickory, Indian Creek, and other places encouraged the growth of these truck farms. The railroad

The Jolliff United Methodist Church in Western Branch has roots that go back to c. 1798, when it was known as the Jolliff meeting house. The present building was erected c. 1850 and has been remodeled several times.

carried tons of locally raised farm produce to town before a combination of good roads and motor trucks began to compete for this business.

The importance of the church to the Western Branch community cannot be overstated. The church was not only the center of religious devotion but social life as well. In 1738, the Glebe Church was built a little to the west of the area. The Churchland Baptist Church, established in 1785, was originally called the Shoulder's Hill Baptist Church and was located in old Nansemond County about midway between Portsmouth and Suffolk. In 1829, a second building was erected on Sycamore Hill, and it was then that the name was changed to Churchland Baptist Church. The Jolliff United Methodist Church, which was originally known as the Jolliff Meeting House, was founded in 1798; however, the present church was constructed around 1850. The Jolliff Methodist Church is one of the original churches in the Western Branch Borough and was located on "The Road," which in colonial times was the main route from Suffolk to Portsmouth and is known today as Jolliff Road.

Attracted by the lure of rich farming land at reasonable prices around 1900, a number of families of Polish descent settled in the Bowers Hill–Sunray section of Western Branch. As the community grew and prospered, the first congregation of St. Mary's Catholic Church was established in 1915. Religious affiliations were as varied then as they are today and included Baptists, Methodists, Episcopalians, Catholics, Jews, and other denominations.

Shipbuilding was one of the major industries in this area. Boats were the colonists' main means of transportation and were also used for the shipment of their products. The Norfolk Naval Shipyard, formerly known as the Gosport Navy Yard, has been in existence since November 1, 1767. It started as a private business and later became a government shipyard. It is especially remembered for the first drydock in America and as the building site of the Confederate ironclad *Virginia*, formerly the *Merrimac*. Shipbuilding was done all along the waterfront, but in the 1890s, the largest shipbuilding area was located at Lovett's Point.

The War Between the States came to Norfolk County and played a big part in the history of Western Branch. A fort known as the Forrest Entrenchment lies in Western Branch. Next to the fort is Goose Creek, and across the street from the fort lie the ruins of Hall's gristmill. Close to this old fort is the Bowers Hill railhead. The primary reasons for building Forrest Entrenchment were to protect the railhead and the mill at Hall's Corner.

During World War II, women began working at the shipyards, naval bases, and other industries. Craney Island was and still is a Navy refueling station. What is now Tidewater Community College (TCC-Portsmouth campus) was an ammunition depot known as "Pig Point." Marines were transported there from Parris Island, South Carolina, for shipment overseas. There was a prisoner-of-war camp at Thalia near Rosmont Road in Virginia Beach, and the German prisoners there were bused daily to Western Branch farms to work.

The Western Branch section of Chesapeake has had many different railroads in the last 150 years. The Seaboard Railroad was rolling into Portsmouth, and the

Atlantic Coastline was going north through Suffolk to Richmond. The Atlantic and Danville Railroad (A&D) ran from the Shoulder's Hill area to First Street in Portsmouth by the Norfolk Naval Shipyard.

The Western Branch Railroad connected Pinner's Point, Virginia, and the car ferry slips of the New York, Philadelphia, & Norfolk railroads to the truck farms in Norfolk and Nansemond County. Thus, farmers were provided with a direct link to larger markets in the big eastern cities such as New York and Boston.

In the 1880s, a railroad was built along Bruce Road from Portsmouth to Driver. A train station called Bruce Station was constructed on the route and it also served as the post office, which was officially known as Mackie, Virginia. By the 1930s, roads had been improved and railroads expanded their operations, making it more profitable to ship by trucks and trains.

In earlier years, Western Branch was not only known for its vital link in the transportation of produce from the area but also for its fish and oysters. Pollution of the Western Branch of the Elizabeth River has, for the most part, eliminated the waters that once produced an abundance of fish and large, flavorful oysters, which were harvested by local farmers and commercial watermen.

Most of the truck farms that helped feed the people of this area as well as those of other areas have been subdivided and given names such as Silverwood, Poplar

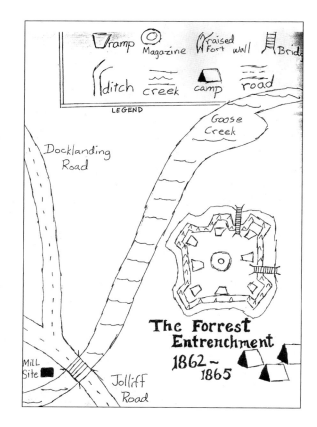

This drawing illustrates the Civil War fort known as the Forrest Entrenchment, which was in what is now the Western Branch community of Chesapeake.

Hill, Dunedin, and Green Meadow Point. The trains no longer take on passengers, and the streetcar has since stopped running from downtown Portsmouth to Churchland.

Western Branch, like other parts of Norfolk County, fought to avoid annexation by surrounding cities. In the 1950s, high taxes contributed to the disappearance of truck farms. The farmers could no longer afford the land taxes, and so they sold out to developers.

Residents of Portsmouth soon began moving to the more peaceful neighborhoods of Western Branch, and within a few years, its population had almost doubled. Limited access to other areas of Chesapeake was an early problem and even today it is considered a long way from the municipal center at Great Bridge. The people who called Western Branch home before Norfolk County and South Norfolk merged to form Chesapeake in 1963 would hardly recognize it now. The population of Western Branch has nearly tripled since 1970, making it, in terms of population, one of the fastest-growing areas of the city.

When traveling through Western Branch on Interstate I-664, the rural feel of the area with its views of open fields, marshland, and wooded areas influences one's impression of Western Branch. Similar impressions are formed when entering Western Branch from the west along Route 58/460/13 and Portsmouth Boulevard (Route 337). Natural features are likewise highlighted by scenic vistas of the Elizabeth River. The river and its tributary streams serve to define and group neighborhood clusters within the area and thus contribute to a community feeling.

The U.S. steam frigate Franklin *is shown anchored off Gosport, c. 1878. The Gosport Navy Yard was later renamed the Norfolk Navy Yard and Gosport eventually became part of the city of Portsmouth.*

7. Deep Creek and the Dismal Swamp

When Deep Creek is mentioned, many people think of the Dismal Swamp, with its canal and locks. They may even remember the antebellum homes and churches in the area, but the section has a fascinating colonial-era history as well.

The Deep Creek settlement got its name from its waterway, the mouth of which is part of the Southern Branch of the Elizabeth River and which was discovered by early colonists from Jamestown. They found that it could easily accommodate large boats to the swamp and the thousands of trees that could provide lumber for building ships. The harvesting of lumber caused people to settle on the fringes of the swamp—most of them living at the village of Deep Creek. The settlement was the halfway point between Jamestown and North Carolina. During colonial times, it has been said that Deep Creek had at least four hotels and a tavern to accommodate travelers on their way to North Carolina.

During the seventeenth and eighteenth centuries, religious persecution existed in the colony of Virginia. The Church of England was the established church, and dissenters were not welcome. Prior to the Revolution, there were Baptists, Presbyterians, and Methodists living in Virginia, but very few had located in the southeastern section of the colony.

In 1778, Virginia enacted the Statute for Religious Freedom. After that, members of all religious sects were free to practice their own beliefs, and at the close of the Revolution, the number of Baptists, Presbyterians, and Methodists increased greatly. Many of them were baptized in the waters of the Deep Creek in Norfolk County.

Baptists settled in Deep Creek as early as 1785. That year 12 people from that village were received into membership of the new Shoulder's Hill Baptist Church in Nansemond County. One of them, a man named Jeremiah Ritter, later became a minister and served the Shoulder's Hill Church, which later became the Churchland Baptist Church.

Nothing, however, is known after that time of a Baptist Church in Deep Creek until 1830. At that time, the Portsmouth Baptist Association listed a church from that area, with Reverend Jeremiah Hendren as a delegate. Nothing further was heard from the church, and it was dropped from the association in 1840. A report made by the state missionary in 1852 mentioned 32 members of a Baptist Sunday school in Deep Creek. The superintendent was listed as Absolom Cherry. The

This is the village of Deep Creek as it appeared in the early twentieth century. The Deep Creek Baptist Church stands to the left of the main road.

missionary indicated that these persons were eager to form a church, but no church was organized until after the Civil War.

On August 29, 1869, three ministers, Reverend N.B. Cobb, Reverend Harvey Hatcher, and Reverend J.G. Hobday, met in the home of Mrs. Josephine Cherry, and the Deep Creek Baptist Church was formed with 17 charter members. In April 1870, Reverend A. Paul Repiton began serving as the first minister. His salary was $150 per annum.

Construction of a church building was begun in 1871, and in 1875, on the fourth Sunday in April, the edifice was dedicated. Painted a reddish brown in color, it was a rough frame building, erected on land leased from the Lake Drummond Canal and Water Company for 99 years at the rate of $1 per year rental. A lease recorded in the clerk's office of the Circuit Court of the City of Chesapeake lists George W. Brown, E.B. Hurdle, and George W. Culpepper Sr. as trustees of the Deep Creek Baptist Church.

Around 1893, the church was remodeled and a new steeple and bell were added. Baptisms were still conducted in the Deep Creek. In 1925, a baptistery was built in the new church.

Mrs. Mary A. Deal, widow of a charter member and former deacon of the church, broke the ground for a new brick church to be erected on the site of the original building in February 1925. The house of worship, which was dedicated by the state missionary, was constructed at a cost of $32,300. Reverend W.L. Larsen conducted the service in November 1925.

The Deep Creek Baptist Church purchased the land on which the building stood from the U.S. government in the year 1940. The deed was dated November 6, 1940. During the mid-1940s, a brick parsonage was completed, and in 1957, an educational building was erected at a cost of $162,000.

The church on Mill Creek Parkway in Deep Creek has served the residents of Norfolk County and those of the City of Chesapeake for 133 years. Its members have continued their support in the new century.

In the early 1900s, Deep Creek was mostly a farming community. The small number of farming families raised corn, sweet potatoes, Irish potatoes, snap beans, and strawberries. Fresh produce began to replace lumber as the main cargo on the steamboats. The town had only three or four stores, so most shopping was done in Portsmouth. Residents of Gilmerton, which was a town of its own, rode the streetcar to Portsmouth for most of their shopping needs. In 1907, John L. Roper Lumber Company was located in Gilmerton along the Elizabeth River near Deep Creek. There were still a few men employed at the remaining lumber mills.

The local lumber camps, gristmills, wharves, and railroad depot have all disappeared. The *Emma Kay* no longer plows the waters of the Elizabeth River, picking-up passengers on its way to Portsmouth and Norfolk. However, like Western Branch and Great Bridge, the population of Deep Creek has more than doubled since the merger in 1963.

As mentioned, Deep Creek, like many other areas of Norfolk County, depended on farming for its existence. With the Great Depression of 1929 came bank foreclosures, which led to the loss of individual farms. Fewer farms meant less produce for the boats that ran between Norfolk County and the Roanoke

Before baptismal fonts were introduced, church members used to gather for total immersion baptisms in the Deep Creek, like this one from around the turn of the twentieth century.

Docks in Norfolk. Through all of the lean years, logs were still harvested from the Dismal Swamp.

It is believed that the Dismal Swamp was at one time part of the area controlled by Chief Powhatan. The Indians felt that the swamp belonged to the Great Spirit, and because of that, none of the tribes lived inside it. The tribes from the south camped on Smith's Ridge in North Carolina and those to the north and west congregated in the area that is now Deep Creek. From those two locations, the Indians hunted, trapped, and fished in the Great Dismal. They took only what they needed and used all that they took.

Seventeenth-century maps of Lower Norfolk County show areas referred to as "black water," those regions were most likely part of the swamp. Life expectancy in the Chesapeake Bay area was lower than in the northern colonies, and the swamp has been blamed for the unhealthy conditions that existed. While it has never been determined exactly what diseases took the greatest toll, it is certain that dysentery was responsible for many deaths.

Lake Drummond, in the Dismal Swamp, was named for William Drummond, first governor of North Carolina (1663–1667), who discovered the lake on a hunting trip. Only the governor returned from this trip, his three hunting companions perishing in the attempt. Governor Drummond was not privileged to participate in later developments of the swamp, however, as he was hanged about ten years later. In 1676, he was tried and found guilty as a traitor, for he had taken part in Bacon's Rebellion against Governor Sir William Berkeley of Virginia.

The Great Dismal Swamp is covered by a layer of thick spongy vegetation augmented by a growth of aquatic plants, bushes, and timber. Freshwater Lake Drummond lies in the center.

Dismal Swamp received its name from Colonel William Byrd II when he was in the area in 1728. He called it a "frightful place" and found nothing charming about it. The English writer Charles Frederick Stansbury found its moods "as variable as a woman," but admitted "in the early fall when clad in the rainbow tints of changing foliage, it is at its best." This map shows how the swamp straddles the North Carolina–Virginia border.

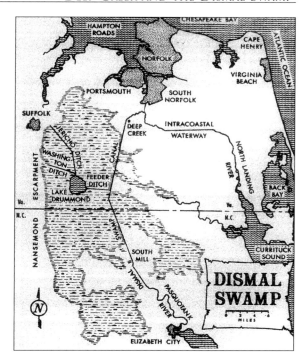

The surface of Lake Drummond is 22 feet above sea level and it is approximately 3 miles in diameter. The original depth was about 15 feet before man began to remove timber and drain the swamp into feeder ditches. This lowered the level and it now averages 6 feet.

When Colonel William Byrd II was in the area in 1728 to survey and run a boundary between the colonies of Virginia and North Carolina, he made many observations of the swamp. He discovered a large area of green cane, which grew 15 feet in height. He gave this the name "Green Sea." Byrd called the great freshwater morass "a frightful place." He found nothing charming about it. He wrote that not even birds would fly over it "for fear of the noisome exhalations that rise from the vast body of dirt and nastiness." Byrd and his party were almost devoured by yellow flies, chiggers, and ticks. The party got lost and ran out of food. These unpleasant experiences, with the difficulties of penetrating the dense jungle, most certainly colored his impressions and partially accounted for the bad report he gave the swamp. For it was Byrd who gave it the name Dismal Swamp.

Unlike Byrd, many found opportunity and inspiration from the Dismal Swamp. In 1803, the popular Irish poet Thomas Moore (1779–1852) visited Lake Drummond and the Dismal Swamp. As the story goes, while sipping suds in a Norfolk tavern, he heard the Indian legend of the lady in the lake. Moore found the lake to be the perfect setting for his piece "A Ballad: The Lake of the Dismal Swamp," which tells of a deranged lover searching for his dead sweetheart whom he imagines lost in the waters of the Dismal Swamp. The famous novelist Harriet

Beecher Stowe (1811–1896) used Virginia's Nat Turner insurrection for her novel *Dred: A Tale of the Dismal Swamp*, written in 1856. On the eve of the Civil War, New England poet Henry Wadsworth Longfellow (1807–1882) wrote of a runaway slave who seeks refuge in the swamp in his poem "The Slave in the Dismal Swamp." David Hunter Strother sketched and wrote about the swamp for Harper's in 1857. Throughout the years, the Dismal Swamp and Lake Drummond have served many writers in a variety of ways and have been responsible for other writings.

While Byrd observed no wildlife in the Dismal Swamp, naturalist Dr. Paul Bartsch, in June 1899, found the swamp filled with musical sounds and listed 52 different kinds of birds observed on two summer trips.

About 35 years after Colonel Byrd's visit, George Washington made his first visit to the swamp in 1763 when he was 31 years old. Washington, with the eye of a hopeful investor, found it a glorious paradise abounding in wild fowl and game. He, as did Byrd, sensed the practical value of connecting Virginia with North Carolina by means of a ship canal and a stage road. Washington made seven trips into the swamp. He has been credited with surveying much of it, but Greshom Nimmo did the actual survey while Washington supervised. Washington is also credited with discovering the headwaters of the Nansemond River.

George Washington, along with Patrick Henry, Thomas and William Nelson, Thomas Walker, Robert Tucker, and others, organized a lumber company called "Adventurers for Draining the Dismal Swamp." The Royal Council of the Virginia Colony granted them 40,000 acres in the swamp. Three years later, Washington and Fielding Lewis acquired an additional 1,100 acres in the Dismal Swamp.

After Washington's death in 1799, his executors purchased his holdings, which remained in possession of Judge Bushrod Washington and his heirs for about 100 years. William N. Camp of Camp Manufacturing Company later purchased the Washington property and it became a part of Union Bag–Camp Manufacturing

Union-Camp owns about half, approximately 50,000 acres, of the Dismal Swamp in Virginia and uses it for production of timber. A large amount of acreage in North Carolina has been reclaimed for agriculture.

William Byrd had first proposed the Dismal Swamp Canal early in the eighteenth century, but it was not authorized by the Virginia General Assembly until 1787 and was ratified by North Carolina in 1790. The Dismal Swamp Canal Company began construction in 1793 at both ends of the proposed cut. The intent was to connect the Southern Branch of the Elizabeth River near Norfolk with the Pasquotank River in Camden County, North Carolina. Because the canal was dug by hand, progress was slow and expenses were high. The cut was completed in 1805 and a toll was placed on the east bank. The canal was 15 feet wide and had two locks. A feeder ditch to Lake Drummond was cut and four locks were added in 1812. Between 1827 and 1829, the waterway was widened and made deeper, and the wooden locks were replaced with locks of stone.

Completion of the Albermarle and Chesapeake Canal in 1858 dealt a serious blow to the Dismal Swamp Canal. During and after the Civil War, the canal became badly deteriorated, and the owners, being nearly bankrupt, sold its interest. The new owner made many improvements between 1896 and 1899 and removed all but two locks. In 1912–1913, the U.S. government purchased the Albemarle and Chesapeake Canal and made it toll-free. The Lake Drummond Canal and Water Company Canal could not compete, and the Dismal Swamp Canal again began to deteriorate. In 1929, the U.S. government bought the Dismal Swamp Canal and began to make improvements. In 1933, the channel was widened and made deeper. In 1933–1934, new drawbridges were built at Deep Creek and South Mills. In 1935, a new control spillway was built at Lake Drummond. In 1940–1941, new locks were built at Deep Creek and South Mills. In 1963–1964, new canal control spillways were built at both ends of the canal. Maintenance dredging is done periodically.

Now on the National Historic Register, the Dismal Swamp Canal is the oldest operating artificial waterway in the country. Both the Albemarle and Chesapeake and the Dismal Swamp Canals are operated by the Army Corps of Engineers and form a part of the Atlantic Intracoastal Waterway.

In 1964, the Chesapeake Chamber of Commerce launched a study to determine the tourist possibilities of the Great Dismal Swamp and to recommend development of facilities there that would help attract visitors. At that time, the State of Virginia was studying possible sites in the swamp for a state forest. A $10,000 grant was made available by the General Assembly for the study. State Senator Gordon F. Marsh sponsored the state study legislation with a view to preserving a wildlife belt in the swamp and to giving the public access to the wildlife treasures of the Great Dismal.

The committee from the chamber worked closely with Fred Heutte, who was the director of the Norfolk Botanical Gardens. Heutte proposed that both banks of the George Washington Canal, which flanks the swamp on the east, be planted as a "horticultural showcase." Heutte's plan was to make the canal a long reflecting garden to serve as a center strip for a new four-lane highway on U.S. 17 flanking both sides of the canal.

Washington's Forest Inc., a land development company, offered to donate half the right of way (21 miles between Deep Creek in Chesapeake and South Mills, North Carolina) for widening U.S. 17. The offer was made by C.T.S. Keep, vice president of the Land Company. The existing two-lane highway ran along the east bank of the canal, while Washington's Forest planned to donate land on the west bank.

The plan called for boat trips on the canal and places to stay, and the revenue was to be used to help maintain the gardens. Another part of the plan was to develop the land on the east side of the highway in nurseries and other businesses and possibly develop a tourist railroad through the swamp. Although there was great interest shown by several organizations, these plans died in the early stages. The main ingredient that would have ensured success was missing—funding.

8. THE MERGER OF SOUTH NORFOLK AND NORFOLK COUNTY

Where did the City of Chesapeake come from? When asked that question, many residents will reply that there has always been a City of Chesapeake or that it is several hundred years old. Technically speaking, that is correct, but the area did not receive the name until January 1, 1963. Prior to that date, it was the City of South Norfolk and the County of Norfolk. The merger of the two entities into a single city became effective on the first day of the new year of 1963.

The next question that may come to mind is "Why the name Chesapeake?" Did the new city receive its name from Chesapeake Avenue in the old City of South Norfolk? The answer is no, and nor did the name come from the Chesapeake Bay.

The merger referendum was held on Tuesday, February 13, 1962, and consolidation was approved. On June 26, 1962, voters went to the polls to select a name for the new city. There were 12 names on the ballot. Of those previously named in the chapter on South Norfolk, the name of Chesapeake received the most votes. The area of Norfolk County had originally been referred to as the land of the Chesapeake because it was where the Chesapeake Indians had made their home.

There was a problem with the selection of the name though, for there already existed a Chesapeake in the state. It was the name of a rural postal station on the Eastern Shore of Virginia. A deputy assistant to the U.S. postmaster general was sent from Washington to settle the conflict, but by the time he arrived, judges of the Circuit Court of Norfolk County and the Corporation Court of South Norfolk had signed orders confirming the results of the referendum. The only way the name could now be changed was through a charter change that required approval by the General Assembly. What ever happened to the other Chesapeake? The use of zone numbers, which preceded zip codes, most likely solved the problem.

If the postal station on Eastern Shore had won, the residents of Chesapeake would now be living in the City of Great Bridge instead of the City of Chesapeake. The name Great Bridge received the second-highest number of votes when the citizens went to the polls to select a name for the new city.

The birth of Chesapeake came five months after voters approved the merger of the two communities. One was a county that throughout the years had lost land, population, and tax dollars to the surrounding cities; the other, a small city plagued by shrinking resources and building room.

In 1961, an amendment to a state law prohibited cities from annexing neighboring cities. Norfolk County political leaders decided to take advantage of the change to stop the massive annexations by the cities of Portsmouth and Norfolk. The politicians from both South Norfolk and Norfolk County met secretly for one year and planned the merger. They did not want their land-hungry neighbors to know about their plans. During the previous dozen or so years, Norfolk County had lost 33 square miles of land, 110,448 residents, $1.88 million in tax revenue, and $92.6 million in taxable property.

Mayor Charles Richardson of South Norfolk and four other council members had agreed to look into the possibility of merging with the county. He stated that the city was small and was having to compete with the larger surrounding cities for teachers, firemen, and policemen. He further stated that it was becoming more difficult to find a place to put the city refuse.

The meetings with Norfolk County began in October 1961 and were held in the secluded county Civic Center in Great Bridge, where a court and city hall complex were under construction. They met behind closed doors in a back room of the Health Department.

At the same time, merger plans were taking place between Princess Anne County and the resort town of Virginia Beach. It has been said that the media in Tidewater was preoccupied with this and none of the negotiations in Norfolk County ever reached the newspapers, radio, or television. This must have been the best-kept secret in the entire state.

Pictured here is Chesapeake's first city council in 1963. Charles L. Richardson, fifth from left, was the last mayor of South Norfolk. Colon L. Hall, to his left, became the first mayor of Chesapeake. Richardson served as Chesapeake's vice mayor.

The meetings were informal and it was decided that if the group were unanimous, it would take further steps toward merger. At the third meeting, they decided to proceed and spokesmen for the two communities contacted the law firm of Hunton, Gay, Williams and Powell in Richmond to begin drafting the merger agreement and a proposed city charter. This firm was also preparing the merger documents for Virginia Beach and Princess Anne County.

Two weeks prior to Christmas 1961, the lawyers completed a proposed charter and a proposed merger agreement, and it was at that time that the information reached the newspapers. During the week before Christmas, the governing bodies of the county and the city held separate public meetings and adopted the charter and merger agreements. There were some minor changes before the petitions were entered in the courts of both communities calling for a referendum to be held in February 1962.

Large full-page advertisements were placed in the local newspapers outlining the merger and charter provisions, and a series of public hearings were scheduled throughout Norfolk County and the City of South Norfolk by proponents of the consolidation.

There were many citizens in opposition to the merger, especially in Western Branch and South Norfolk, and a lot of anger appeared at the public meetings. Some of the residents of Western Branch said that if they merged, they would rather it be with the City of Portsmouth. Those in South Norfolk that opposed the merger predicted that the city would lose everything and would be gobbled up by Norfolk County. Also, a goodly number of South Norfolk citizens could see

This 8-by-14-foot mural, which hangs in Chesapeake's Museum, represents the city of Chesapeake. It was painted by Kenneth Harris, who also designed the city seal pictured at left. The banner at bottom right contains a quote attributed to Colonel William Woodford after the Battle of Great Bridge.

nothing to be gained by merging with the county. After all, South Norfolk was a city of the first class and could not be annexed by any of the surrounding cities.

Among those in South Norfolk who were against the merger were the school board and superintendent of schools, Dr. E.E. Brickell. Dr. Brickell was then and is now a scholarly gentleman who became known throughout the state for his affiliations with the College of William and Mary, the Virginia Beach School System, and the Eastern Virginia Medical School.

The merger won, and the General Assembly granted a charter for the new city shortly afterwards. After the charter was granted and before Chesapeake officially became a city, the governing bodies of the two communities met regularly to prepare for the upcoming transition. Standing committees were created to oversee the formation of various governmental functions. Several departments that had not existed previously had to be created. The county did not have a public works department, so the department was formed, and C.W. Taylor became its head. A planning department was created with Durwood Curling as its head. Curling later served as the city manager of Chesapeake.

At the time of the merger, the population of Norfolk County was 51,000 and that of South Norfolk was 22,000. Debts of the two communities totaled about $22 million each. The county debt was increased by the approval of $3.5 million in bonds for school construction.

The leaders in both communities decided to let the constitutional officers of each area decide among themselves who would head their separate departments. There was some duplication, and only one person could serve as department head. There were two treasurers: Otto Lynch was treasurer of Norfolk County, and N. Duval Flora was treasurer of South Norfolk. Flora became treasurer, and Lynch retired. Peter M. Axson Jr. became the city's first commonwealth attorney, and South Norfolk's William L. Forbes became city attorney. Forbes later became a circuit court judge and was a chief judge when he retired. The commissioner of revenue was Robert H. Waldo of Norfolk County, while Mike Smith from South Norfolk chose to become Waldo's deputy. Arthur Hodges, Norfolk County sheriff, became the new Chesapeake sheriff, while J.K. Holland became Chesapeake's new high constable.

The new Chesapeake City Council consisted of the five members of the South Norfolk Council and the five members of the county board of supervisors, who represented each of the magisterial districts of the county. A tie-breaker was appointed by the Circuit Court to resolve any issue that ended in a deadlock. Otto Lynch was named to this position. Lynch was later succeeded by James N. Garrett Sr., a county attorney.

The South Norfolk representatives to the council were Charles Richardson (South Norfolk mayor), Dan Lindsey, Howard McPherson, H.S. Boyette, and Floyd Allen. Those from Norfolk County included Colon Hall, T. Ray Hassell Jr., I.H. Haywood, G.A. Treakle, and Eugene Wadsworth.

An organizational meeting was held on January 2, 1963, and the council elected Colon Hall as the city's first mayor. Richardson was elected to the position of vice mayor. At this same meeting, Phillip R. Davis, who had served as city manager of South Norfolk, became the first city manager of Chesapeake. His salary was $14,000 per year.

The seat of governmental operations would be the civic center at Great Bridge. Construction of the court and city hall buildings had been completed in October 1962. The county government had met previously at the office of the clerk of the Norfolk County Circuit Court, off High Street in Portsmouth. South Norfolk's council had met for years on the second floor of the municipal building on Liberty Street. This building has since been demolished.

With five members from the South Norfolk council and five from the county's magisterial districts, a power struggle soon developed. The in-fighting reached its peak in 1965 when two South Norfolk councilmen sought to dissolve the merger in the wake of a U.S. District Court order to reapportion council seats on a one-man, one-vote basis. This court action put an end to the five council seats from South Norfolk and was a threat to the political strength of the borough. The court ruling meant that the merger could not be dissolved. In plain words, they were told, "You created it, now make it work."

Chesapeake's first at-large election was held on April 26, 1966, and a nine-man ticket, led by G.A. Treakle, went into office. This election ensured that Norfolk County controlled the city government. Members of the council elected Treakle mayor of the city. The county was now in control, for they not only dominated the city council, but they also held a majority of the seats on the school board. There were 11 members on the school board, 6 were from the county and 5 were from South Norfolk. The school board had been formed under the chairmanship of B.M. Williams, who had been head of the county school board. F.J. Richardson, chairman of the South Norfolk School Board, became vice chairman. The new superintendent of schools in Chesapeake was Edwin W. Chittum, who had been the county school superintendent since 1949.

When the clock struck midnight on December 31, 1962, Chesapeake officially became a city, with 363,450 square miles of land and a population of more than 75,000. It was the fifth largest city in land area in the nation. Before the merger, Portsmouth had filed an annexation suit against Norfolk County for 44.7 square miles of land in Western Branch and Deep Creek. Three days after the new city was born, a three-court judge ruled that the annexation suit was still active. For the next four years, Chesapeake and Portsmouth were in court over this land, population, and taxes. In 1967, the three-member Circuit Court panel awarded Portsmouth 10.45 square miles of Chesapeake and 11,822 of its residents. Most of the land was in the Churchland area of Western Branch. Chesapeake's losses also included three schools, 45 miles of sewer and water lines, a library branch, a fire station, and the West Norfolk Bridge.

The court ordered Portsmouth to pay Chesapeake $10.9 million. The money was used to help pay for capital improvements, which included a sewer and water system, four new schools, street and highway improvements, and a main library.

Voters approved a $26.5 million bond referendum in November 1969. This allowed the city to extend its water lines and to finance its own water system. The opening of the Northwest River water treatment plant in 1979 marked another step towards independence from the surrounding cities. Until then, local water resources had been totally controlled by the cities of Norfolk and Portsmouth. The plant was initially designed to supply up to 10 million gallons a day to city customers. Another event of importance was the opening of the $10 million high-rise bridge over the Southern Branch of the Elizabeth River in 1965. It was the last segment of the Interstate 64 construction project that linked Chesapeake residents with Norfolk, Portsmouth, Virginia Beach, and Suffolk.

It has been just a little over 39 years since a large part of what is now Chesapeake consisted of farms and woodlands. Chesapeake has had its share of growing pains, but today it is a large sprawling city with a growing population.

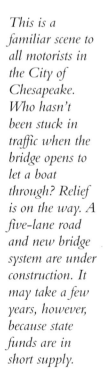

This is a familiar scene to all motorists in the City of Chesapeake. Who hasn't been stuck in traffic when the bridge opens to let a boat through? Relief is on the way. A five-lane road and new bridge system are under construction. It may take a few years, however, because state funds are in short supply.

9. Early Tidewater Religions

The first report of religion in the area was found in a legal document dated May 15, 1637, when mention was made of an Anglican parish in Lower Norfolk County. The Anglican Church was the Church of England and under instructions dated July 24, 1621, the governor was required to keep up the religion of the Church of England in the Colony of Virginia.

Today, the City of Chesapeake has within its boundaries more than 50 different denominations. Even with this large variety of churches, the main religions include Baptist, Methodist, Presbyterian, Lutheran, Congregational Christian, and Roman Catholic. The Jewish population attends services in Portsmouth or Norfolk.

Before the American Revolution, the Church of England was the predominant church in the colonies. What was then known as the Anglican Church became the Episcopal Church. The first church in the Anglican parish was constructed at Lynnhaven in 1638. There are now four Episcopal Churches in Chesapeake.

The first church in what is now Chesapeake was established in 1639, but was not built until 1661. It was a chapel of ease for the Elizabeth River Parish, and it was located on the Southern Branch of the Elizabeth River between Jones Creek and Scuffletown Creek in South Norfolk. Called the Southern Branch Chapel, it was moved in 1701 to Great Bridge and was located at the southwest corner of what is now Battlefield Boulevard and Cedar Road. In April 1728, it was still called the Southern Branch Chapel, but by October 1749, according to records, it was known as the Great Bridge Chapel. In 1750 it was enlarged, and in 1752 a well was dug on the property.

The chapel was the victim of considerable damage from cannon fire during the Revolutionary War, especially during the battle of Great Bridge. The 2nd Virginia Regiment had used it as a fort. It is not known for sure, but apparently the chapel was not abandoned and dismantled until 1845, after having once again become a chapel of ease, this time serving the St. Brides Parish.

St. Brides, which included all the county south of the Eastern Branch of the Elizabeth River and east of the Southern Branch, was established in 1761. St. Brides Church, sometimes called the Northwest Church, was built in 1762 and remained in the area until 1853. James Pasteur was its first minister and he served from 1761 to 1774. John Portlock and William Smith, according to a deed of 1763, were the first churchwardens, and Malachi Wilson and William Happer were named in a deed dated 1768. The names of the 12 vestrymen are listed in a Norfolk County court order of 1761.

The church, or the chapel, was not used much after the Revolution. Reverend John H. Rowland, who was minister in 1775, was a Loyalist and was reported to have assisted Lord Dunmore with information about the activities of his parishioners. Because of his loyalty to the crown, his congregation became permanently alienated from the church. It is not known if Rowland was tarred and feathered and run out of town, but historians have said that he went to New York, where he became chaplain for the Loyalist 2nd Battalion of New Jersey Volunteers.

Captain James Wilson, a vestryman in 1761, gave land to be used for construction of the Hickory Grove Methodist Church, which was founded in 1790. This is now the Hickory United Methodist Church.

In 1911, the Episcopalians built a church at the corner of Dinwiddie Street and Poplar Avenue in the Berkley section of Norfolk and gave it the name St. Brides. In 1923, St. Brides Church merged with another Episcopal Church, and in 1960, they moved to the 600 block of Sparrow Road, which is now part of Chesapeake. This church is responsible for starting St. Thomas Church in Great Bridge. St. Thomas was a mission in 1956 but became an independent parish on January 20, 1975.

The Puritan (Protestant) movement in England was responsible for the rise of several denominations, which included Presbyterians, Methodists, and Baptists. It was during the Civil War in England when the Roundheads were pitted against

The Rosemont Christian Church was organized on August 14, 1902. The church shown here is the third building and was constructed in 1931 under the pastorate of Reverend Joseph Franklin Morgan, shown to the right of the entrance.

the monarchy that Presbyterianism became the legal form of ecclesiastical government in the established church.

Presbyters (priests or elders) governed the individual churches as opposed to the episcopal form of government, where a diocese comes under the jurisdiction of a bishop. Presbyterizing of the church was brought to the American colonies as early as 1645, and a minister from the Elizabeth River parish was dismissed because he favored it. Some colonies welcomed Puritans, while others dismissed them. This nonconformity continued in Norfolk County even after the monarchy was restored in 1660. The Presbyterian denomination was strengthened by an influx of Scots both before and after the Revolutionary War. There are about ten Presbyterian Churches in Chesapeake at this time.

Methodism arrived in Norfolk County about 1770. At that time, a Mr. Cutherell opened his home in Great Bridge to friends and relatives so that they might meet in the Methodist manner for singing and praying. It was a revival movement within the Anglican Church. The Cutherell home, which was destroyed by fire in the mid-1800s, was less than a mile from where the present-day Oak Grove Methodist Church stands. It was in 1763 that people from Norfolk County went to Portsmouth to hear their Methodist preachers and in 1772 to hear preaching in Norfolk.

On August 10, 1772, Joseph Pilmoor, a famous Methodist preacher, left Norfolk and traveled to Great Bridge, where he spoke to a group at the home of a Mr. Manning. Pilmoor later returned to Norfolk County and preached at Western Branch, Grassfield, and Indian River. He organized a Methodist society at New Mill Creek and revisited it on April 14, 1773. Other Methodist ministers

Lake Drummond Baptist Church, seen here, is located at 3873 Ballahack Road. The church, which was completed in 1851, was built on land donated by Michael Sykes.

that preached in Norfolk County included William Watters, Robert Williams, Francis Asbury, and Edward Bailey.

On February 11, 1804, Bennett Armstrong and his wife, Jinny, donated one-half acre of land, about a mile from where the Oak Grove Church is now located, for the building a Methodist Episcopal church. The first Methodist church was built on this site about four or five years later. It has been said that the old Cutherell meeting house was moved on rollers, probably logs, to the present site of the Oak Grove Church in 1842.

During the Civil War, a nearby family hid the communion silver, carpet, and the church Bible in their home for safe keeping before the Yankees arrived. After the war, the church and the people were impoverished. One week in 1872, only nine people attended church and the collection was 14¢. In 1869, the church had 76 members, and in 1900, it had 72 on roll. After those hard times, the church membership began to grow, and in 1962, the congregation helped start the Great Bridge Methodist Church. Most congregations at this time were without much hard cash, but there were some areas of Norfolk County that were hardly touched by the war. The history of those areas during Reconstruction tells of relative ease and plenty.

The Baptists established the Blackwater Church in 1774 and began their first church in Norfolk County in 1782. The church was called the Upper Bridge Church and later the Northwest River Bridge Church. Today, it is the Northwest Baptist Church and is located at 848 Ballahack Road. In the beginning, it was served by itinerant preachers, and its first regular preacher was Elder Jacob Grigg, who remained there until 1802. In 1803, Elder Dempey Casey became pastor of its 52 members. In 1818, the original meeting house was destroyed by fire. A new building was completed in 1821 and its present name was adopted at that time.

The Northwest Church was responsible for establishing two other early Baptist churches. They were Pleasant Grove, founded in 1845, and Lake Drummond Baptist Church, in 1850.

The Churchland Baptist Church was formed in old Nansemond County in 1785 as Shoulder's Hill Baptist Church. It moved 6 miles into Western Branch in 1829, at which time it became known as Sycamore Hill Baptist Church. It is now located at 3031 Churchland Boulevard.

After the Civil War, many other Baptist Churches came into being in what is now the City of Chesapeake; included among these are Centerville Baptist Church, in 1872; Elizabeth River, in 1873; South Norfolk Baptist, in 1893; and Raleigh Heights, in 1897.

The Great Bridge Congregational Christian Church was founded in 1859, when a small group of Christians built a meeting house for worship. The little church, renovated in 1905 as a chapel, was built from hand-hewn timbers. The logs were so solid that, until destroyed by fire in 1973, the structure had been used by all subsequent generations of the church's members and by the Roman Catholic Prince of Peace Mission from 1971 until it built its own structure in 1977. Hurricane Barbara toppled the steeple of the church in October 1953.

In this May 1957 photograph taken from Battlefield Boulevard, the steeple of the Berea Christian Church can be seen in the distance.

The timbered church, called the Methodist Protestant Church at Berea in those days, had earlier survived the ravages of the Civil War. In 1861, it fell into the hands of Union troops and was converted into a horse stable.

In 1870, Berea Church turned down a proposal to go along with a union of the Methodist Protestant and Methodist Episcopal Churches in Virginia. Instead, the church voted in August 1871 to transfer to the Christian Church. It was not until 1955 that it changed its name from Berea Church to the Great Bridge Congregational Christian Church. When the Congregational Christian Churches and the Evangelical and Reform Churches united to become the United Church of Christ, Great Bridge voted to join in the union. Growth was so great that the church was forced to build a new sanctuary, which was dedicated on December 9, 1962.

When the merger took place in 1963, there was one Roman Catholic Church in the new city. The first Catholic Church, St. Mary's at Sunray in the Bower's Hill section, was founded in 1912 by two dozen Polish families who immigrated here between 1908 and 1912. St. Therese's Roman Catholic Church was founded in Portsmouth in 1954, but moved into Chesapeake in 1972. Prince of Peace began meeting in the chapel of Great Bridge Congregational Christian Church on Easter Sunday in 1971. It was founded first as a mission of St. Matthew's Church, which started in Berkley and is now in Virginia Beach. Today it has its own church at 621 Cedar Road. Other Catholic Churches in Chesapeake include St. Stephen Martyr, Robert E. French, St. Benedict's Chapel, and Tridentine Rite Chapel.

It was in 1895 that a Mennonite family by the name of Swartz and two other families from Michigan settled in Norfolk County. In 1910, the agriculture-oriented religious group built the Mount Pleasant Mennonite Church at 2041 Mount Pleasant Road. Other Mennonites from Pennsylvania and Maryland later joined them. Modern life has encroached upon their time-honored farming vocation, and many have entered other fields of employment. Residential and commercial development has led to prosperity for some of Chesapeake's Mennonite families. Some have entered the fields of medicine and law and others have moved to other parts of the country.

The Lutherans arrived in Chesapeake in 1964. Until recent times, the Lutheran Church was mainly an immigrant church, following the German and Scandinavian migration to America. The Lutherans were in the valley of Virginia during colonial times; however, it was on May 20, 1894, that the First Lutheran Church was established in Norfolk. It was located on Colley Avenue. In 1908, the First Lutheran Church in Portsmouth was located at Washington and King Streets. There are now three Lutheran Churches in Chesapeake; they are Apostles Lutheran Church, Faith Evangelical Lutheran Church, and Rejoice Lutheran Church.

There are many other churches in this large, populous City of Chesapeake. Those that have been highlighted here are representative of the earlier religions in the area. The Lutheran Church was included to show that the history of religion in Chesapeake is still being written. In early Norfolk County and in South Norfolk most of the community activities revolved around the churches. They were not only places of worship but also places of entertainment. When there was no place of worship within traveling distance, members of the community, sometimes with the help of an established church, came together to build one.

This photograph, which highlights the Chesapeake Avenue United Methodist Church and the brick sidewalk in the historic district, was taken from a prone position by Kathy Keeney.

10. INDIAN RIVER AND OAKLETTE

A lot of the following information about Oaklette was available due to the foresight of Joseph Paxson, who kept a very accurate account of important events that took place during his life, and to the Committee on History of the Oaklette Methodist Church.

The land in this section of the City of Chesapeake was at one time, as were others nearby, predominately woodlands and fields with farmhouses scattered along the banks of the Indian River. It is not known exactly when Oaklette received its name. Approximately 121 acres of land bounded by the Indian River on the north and on the east and by farms on the west and south is recorded as Oaklette in a deed transfer dated January 24, 1843. Mary Tatem inherited this land from her father, Nathaniel Tatem, in 1836. In 1843, she and her husband, Thomas, sold the land known as Oaklette to John Hope for the sum of $2,100. This land changed hands several times between 1843 and 1869 until Colonel William Etheridge sold it to Matthew Hare of New York. At that time, the deed still referred to the land as Oaklette.

The farms were pretty much isolated at that time, with dirt paths connecting the fields of neighboring farms. Travel was by horse and wagon or buggy, and the nearest main roads were Campostella and Providence. Campostella Road ran from Norfolk to Great Bridge, and Providence Road continued on to the area known as Kempsville. The Providence Christian Church was situated at the intersection of Campostella and Providence Roads. When inclement weather prevailed, the roads became very muddy; wagons usually got stuck and individuals found themselves in mud up to their knees. Oyster shells, when available, were used to cover the roads.

The most desirable mode of travel was by boat, and numerous wharves could be found along the banks of the Indian River. Boats were still being used to ship farm produce to Norfolk and other areas. The waters were still clean, and there was an abundance of fish and oysters, which along with fresh produce from the farms, made for many delightful dinners.

Indian River Road was one of those paths that was occasionally paved with shells from the oysters harvested out of the Indian River. The road became a main thoroughfare when the Indian River Turnpike and Toll Bridge Company was formed, the outfit purchased a 40-foot-wide strip of land between Steamboat

This modern painting portrays a typical farmhouse of the late eighteenth century, based on information from various sources. It was located on the Indian River Branch and was built mostly of hand-hewn heart pine timbers fastened with wooden pegs and handmade nails.

Creek and Sparrow Road in 1878 and created the Indian River Turnpike around 1880. The designation as a turnpike did not mean that the road would necessarily be improved but that a toll could be collected for use of the road. Joseph Paxson, the toll collector, wrote in 1904 and 1905 that the road was in such poor condition that people were refusing to pay the toll. The Turnpike Company went into receivership, and the courts condemned the turnpike as unfit for collection of tolls.

In the early 1900s, Indian River and most of the surrounding communities experienced a considerable amount of growth. Industries were popping up in nearby Berkley and all along the Southern Branch of the Elizabeth River. Paxson recorded in his diary that, by 1902, a few homes in the Oaklette section of Indian River were beginning to be wired for telephones by Southern Bell. In 1904, the Suburban Railroad Company laid tracks from Campostella Heights up to and down Webster Avenue and up Oaklette Avenue to Indian River Turnpike at the bridge. The residents were now able to travel between Norfolk and Oaklette by electric trolley.

With the installation of the trolley, a new bridge was required to accommodate the tracks as well as foot and wagon traffic. On Thursday, November 10, 1904, the first of the pilings was driven. A new steel draw for the bridge arrived by barge in January 1905, and the new bridge was opened for team traffic on March 20, 1905.

Workers then began to remove part of the old draw and bridge so that they could swing the new draw around. The first trolley, number 8, crossed the new bridge on March 22, 1905, at 3:15 p.m.

After the trolley, electric lights came to the area, and Mr. Paxson reported having paid $19 to have his house wired for nine lights and the post office next door wired for one light. On Wednesday, September 6, 1905, electric lamps were installed along the trolley line at the crossroads and curves and on the bridge.

The Oaklette Methodist Church Community Center was probably built between 1884 and 1889 and was located between the church and parsonage. The community as well as the church used this building for socials and meetings. The Oaklette School, which opened in 1900, used this one-room structure and became known as School Number 8 in the Norfolk County School District. It operated there until 1912, when the Norfolk Highlands School was built.

In 1920, a teacher earned $87.50 a month, and for that amount, she was required to teach two grades and perform other duties about the school. Female teachers could not be married, and those from out of town received room and board from local families. The marriage rule was relaxed during World War II but was enforced again when the war ended. Each school year began with a new bottle of ink for the inkwell, which was a hole cut in the top of each desk, and students in the lower grades learned to write by practicing ovals and push-pulls in their Locker Writing books.

Before schools had cafeterias, children brought their lunch in paper bags or lunch buckets. Those who lived within walking distance went home for lunch. When arriving early or during recess, the children played on the school ground. A hand bell was rung several times a day to signal the beginning and ending of the school day, recess, lunch break, and other times as necessary. All of the early schools were heated by a coal furnace, which was located in the basement or on the ground floor.

The students attended the Norfolk Highlands School until they completed the seventh grade. Those who went on to high school rode the bus to Portlock High School, where they graduated after completion of the eleventh grade. The twelfth grade was not added until 1946.

The Norfolk Highland School has received several renovations throughout the years and has come a long way from the one-room building of 1900. The main entrance has been changed from Lilac Avenue to Myrtle Avenue, and the school building has been doubled in size.

Another place of interest in the Oaklette section was the estate of W.W. Colonna Sr. One day, Captain Will Colonna Sr., president of Colonna's Shipyard in Berkley, paddled his canoe 3 miles east up the Elizabeth River where he came upon this beautiful real estate. His remark was that "this is the most beautiful point of land I have ever seen." The next day, he decided to find the owner and see if that person would sell the land. Captain Colonna got into his automobile and drove to the Oaklette section of Norfolk County, where he located Russell Hare, owner of the property. Hare said that he would sell but made it clear that he would sell the entire 20-acre farm, not just the good farm land leaving him with that "no good point of land on the water where the wind always blew the crops down." Captain Colonna agreed and bought the farm, including that "no good point of land on the water" for $10,000. The land included a house that was sitting on the point. The Colonna family lived there while the big house was under construction. This area became known as the "little circle." At that time, the roads from the shipyard were unpaved and nearly unusable even in dry weather. To help solve his transportation problem, Captain Colonna used his speedboat to travel to and from work. Upon completion of the new house, the older home was rolled on pine logs to its new location at 935 St. Lawrence Drive.

In 1920, Captain Colonna designed and built a 48-room mansion on this 20-acre point of land overlooking the Indian River, which is a part of the Eastern Branch of the Elizabeth River. The house was a large wood frame structure standing two full stories with a finished attic and dormers, which made it appear to be three stories high. The living room was 24 by 48 feet, the ceiling was 12 feet high, and all the furniture was Chippendale. There were seven bathrooms and ten fireplaces and the floors were of white oak. There was a below-ground basement that contained a large coal-fired furnace, which supplied hot water for domestic needs and hot water for the cast-iron radiator

The one-room Oaklette School was built between 1884 and 1889. It also served as a community center and, in 1900, became School Number 8 in the Norfolk County District.

The 48-room W.W. Colonna Sr. home was built in 1920 on a 20-acre point of land overlooking the Indian River.

heating system throughout the house. A dumbwaiter took supplies from the basement to the two floors above—with an occasional child catching a ride just for the fun of it.

Construction of the house took one year and cost $126,000, with $78,000 worth of furniture. Access to the house was through large, brick columns and down a lane with lightposts leading to and around a big circle to the main entrance. On the approach to the main entrance, but several hundred feet away, nestled among the pine trees, was a steel water tower, which stood 72 feet high. This, along with a deep well and an electric pump, furnished water to the main house, the guest house, the home of the caretaker, and all other locations on the property that required water.

The caretaker's home was located on the left, or west side, of the property between the lane and the water tower. It was a one-story white wood frame structure with a garage and workshop to the right.

Rocks that had been used as ballast from old sailing vessels were used to construct a walk around the water's edge, a rock garden, and a house. A pond was built off the back of the rock house; its purpose was to contain the water from the river. The pond was large enough that it held five wooden rowboats, one for each girl in the family, and each boat, which was 8 feet in length, was also personalized. The walk continued around the point where there were several sets of steps, some of which were covered with rose trellises and contained flowerpots made of rocks at the entrances. There were wooden seats built around some of the large trees and swings for the children. A pigeon house was perched near the top of a tall tree.

The walk came to an end on the east side of the estate where a huge wire enclosure had been built and was the home of all kinds and sizes of birds, both native and imported.

There was a boat pier at the end of the property where Colonna kept his yacht, which he had named *Margaret*, for his mother. The boat was of such size and complexity that it required an engineer when underway.

A tall flagpole stood at the end of the point, where the American flag was always flown. The concrete foundation contained the footprints of four of Colonna's daughters. Midway on the property was a guest apartment with a car garage underneath and a rose-covered trellis dance hall off the back. There was also a very big stone basket in front where flowers were planted in such a manner that it appeared as a basket of flowers. On the east side of the property and several hundred feet from the bird cage was a doll house with miniature furniture. This is where the girls spent a lot of time playing house.

In addition to all the trees that were on the property when Captain Colonna bought it, there were 101 pecan trees that he purchased through the mail from the state of Georgia. These he planted throughout the property, and most every fall, there was a large harvest of nuts, which the children picked up from the ground.

In the early days of radio, Captain Colonna had a room in the house where people would gather just to listen. He would sometimes place the radio on the porch enabling a much larger group to enjoy the broadcast.

The mansion was typical of that era when many large homes were built. Taxes were few and people were able to keep most of their hard-earned money. Only the very rich made enough to pay any taxes at all. Just after World War I, the expression was "let the good times roll." This was a period of national prosperity, and there was no reason to believe that it would ever come to an end, but it did when the stock market crashed and the Great Depression came. The expression then changed to "Mister, can you spare a dime?"

The house burned twice—the first time was in 1923, when it burned partially and was rebuilt with a flat roof. It has been said that it never looked the same after this fire and the repairs that followed. The second time it burned was on a cold winter night in 1925. This occurred while the family was attending a silent movie at a theater in downtown Norfolk. The fire department was unable to extinguish the fire because the river was frozen and at low tide. In those days, the fire department fought fire by placing suction hoses in the river. Captain Colonna often said that both fires were set and that he knew who did it but there was no way of proving it.

As the house burned, the Colonna children remembered that the family cat had been left in the house while they were away. That night, along with the great sorrow of seeing their beautiful home destroyed, their thoughts turned to the loss of the family pet. Bright and early the next morning, the cat was found wandering around the smoldering ashes. She was totally unharmed. The belief is that when the arsonist went in to start the fire, the cat came out or was put outside by the person or persons that started the blaze.

There was very little insurance on the house. In those days, most people carried very little or no insurance on their homes. The house was not rebuilt after the second fire; however, the property remains in the family to this day and some new things have been added. One addition is a substantial log cabin down near the river.

In 1927, Captain Colonna, with the assistance of his daughters, built a houseboat on an existing Chesapeake & Ohio wooden railroad pontoon, which dated back to the late 1800s. The houseboat was to be used as a hunting lodge. Each year in the late 1920s and early 1930s, the lodge was towed by tugboat to Mill Tail Creek, Buffalo City, North Carolina. It was there that friends and associates hunted deer, bear, and squirrel and counted the liquor stills in the East Lake area.

In 1935, the houseboat was anchored in the Indian River when a violent hurricane broke the boat's anchor cable and blew it up the creek. Captain Colonna built a series of dams and ponds and attempted to float the boat back to the river. After doing this several times and moving the boat a few hundred feet closer to the river, he abandoned the idea. It now remains secure on the bottom of a freshwater pond behind the last dam built by the captain. Today, the houseboat is used for small socials with family, friends, clubs, and business associates. The interior is a mixture of nautical and 1920s furnishings. It even has its own player piano with lots of tunes from the early 1900s, and some very large turtles make their homes in the surrounding waters.

After the second fire in 1925, Captain Will Colonna and his family lived at his lodge in Blackwater, which was in old Princess County on Blackwater Creek. They eventually moved back to Oaklette and lived at the home at 831 St. Lawrence Drive in what is now Chesapeake. Captain Colonna spent the rest of his 94 years there. He often said near his death in January 1977 that had he not smoked he would have lived to 100.

Captain Will Colonna Sr. and his daughters built this houseboat in 1927. It now sits on the bottom of a freshwater pond at the foot of Seneca Avenue.

11. THE NEW CITY OF CHESAPEAKE

At the time of this writing, the City of Chesapeake is in its 39th year, but in reality it goes back much further than 1963, when Norfolk County and the City of South Norfolk merged.

There are landmarks and communities that date back to around 1620. It was in 1661 when the first Southern Branch Chapel was built that written records began to be kept. Many of those early records are still on file in the office of the clerk of the Circuit Court. According to family records, the first John Portlock arrived in the area in 1685; however, it is believed that other members of his family may have visited the colony as early as 1634. So you see, even though the city has technically been in existence only 39 years, parts of it are very old.

The population at the time of the merger was approximately 75,000; today, the city can boast of a population of about 205,000 and it is still growing. The needs and desires of the citizens are many. But how big is too big? Services such as schools, roads, transportation, public safety, medical, and places to shop are among the bare necessities.

One of the first and most basic things needed by all citizens is a mailing address. E. Trigg Harrison became the city's first postmaster in late 1963 when the city was less than a year old. Prior to the formation of the City of Chesapeake, each area had its own hand stamp, which was used as its postmark. Bowers Hill, Hickory, Fentress, St. Brides, Deep Creek, Great Bridge, Buell, Portlock Station, and Camden Mills are examples of stations that had their own rubber stamp. Camden Mills later became Bells Mill, and Buell became Portlock Station.

Beginning in 1884, postboxes (or mailboxes) were installed on several corners throughout small towns and cities. They were mounted on concrete posts, and the boxes, painted olive drab, had a small slot at the top with instructions to "pull down." Home delivery of the mail was made twice a day, six days a week.

Sunday deliveries were made the week before Christmas, and the post office department hired additional personnel to work during the busy month of December. It was a great way to earn college tuition for many. The main post office on Battlefield Boulevard was dedicated in 1967. Although the post office is still there, a new main station has been built on Johnstown Road.

CHESAPEAKE GENERAL HOSPITAL

Mayor Linwood L. Briggs and members of the South Norfolk City Council recognized the need for a hospital back in the 1950s, but their plans were not realized before the merger took place. Shortly after the merger, in the early 1960s, the story of Chesapeake General Hospital began. It was a tremendous community effort that was led by Dr. W. Stanley Jennings. Jennings stated that "We had waiting lists to get our patients into the Norfolk hospitals, so it seemed logical that we needed one in our own backyard. The public was fantastic in their support, but the big guys looked at the hospital as a financial burden that would fall on their shoulders."

Donald S. Buckley, the first and only president of Chesapeake General, started with 35 acres of woodland and a blank sheet of paper. The plan was to have a 141-bed hospital. Twenty-five years later, the hospital and its health family boasts a 260-bed hospital, one assisted living facility and another in the making, two fitness facilities, and home health care and medical office buildings. In 1986, Chesapeake General added a birthing unit. The "BirthPlace" opened with 10 obstetricians on staff delivering 100 babies a month. Today, the hospital has 60 obstetricians and has nearly tripled the number of births per month. In 1995, the Sidney M. Oman Cancer Treatment Center opened. Sidney Oman is a cancer survivor and former mayor of Chesapeake and Elizabeth City, North Carolina.

A new ambulatory care center was dedicated on April 12, 2001. The hospital also operates a 24-hour medical facility on the Outer Banks of North Carolina. In addition, Chesapeake Health has joined with University Health Systems of Eastern Carolina to construct "The Outer Banks Hospital in Dare County."

On Thursday, April 12, 2001, the W. Stanley Jennings Outpatient Center was dedicated. The two-story, $7.5-million building is located just north of the main facility. It was designed so that there will be plenty of natural light throughout the structure. This building is a stand-alone structure and is self contained so that the patients will not have to go through the main hospital. The outpatient center is part of a $30-million expansion and renovation program that will add a women's health care unit and a three-story addition to the main facility. Chesapeake General Hospital celebrated its 25th anniversary with a rededication ceremony on Sunday, January 28, 2001.

CHESAPEAKE LIBRARY SYSTEM

Another success story is that of the Chesapeake Library System, which consists of the Central Library at 298 Cedar Road, five area libraries, and a bookmobile. The area libraries are Indian River, Russell Memorial, Greenbrier, Major Hillard, and the South Norfolk Memorial Library.

The libraries are education support centers in that they provide reference materials as well as computer services. They also have a large collection of recently published novels for the reading enjoyment of citizens of all ages. The Wallace

Chesapeake General Hospital began in the 1960s with 35 acres of woodlands and has grown continuously since that time. This building was completed in 1976.

Room at the Central Library serves as a reference center for genealogical and local history information. There is also a Public Law Library on the second floor. All of Chesapeake's libraries are equipped with videos, magazines, newspapers, and CDs. There are meeting rooms available at each location and are free of charge to non-profit and civic organizations. The system offers reading and other programs for children and adults.

The Friends of the Library hold book sales and are involved in other activities to help the library system financially. Rooms such as the Wallace Room at the Central Library and the Linwood L. Briggs Literacy Room at the South Norfolk Library were made possible by donations from those families. The library sponsors such events as the Senior Citizen art show (usually held during January), Train Time, Civil War Days (held the weekend after Labor Day each year), and Sheep to Shawl (held during National Library Week in late November). These events are carried out at the Central Library.

GREENBRIER FARMS

One of the largest operations in Norfolk County, which carried over into the City of Chesapeake, was that of Greenbrier Farms. In 1914, R.E. Thrasher, an expert in plant life, came to Norfolk County from Greenbrier County, West Virginia. It was from that county that the local farms received their name.

Thrasher had performed a nationwide search of soils and climates best suited for growing a large variety of plants. The land he purchased was a swamp, but

The central library is in the upper right of this view of the Chesapeake municipal center at Great Bridge. The tall building at right center is city hall, the planetarium is in the lower right, and the white building in upper left is the Juvenile and Domestic Relations Court.

with the expenditure of countless hours of labor by a man with a dream, it became a thing of beauty and symmetry. What in the beginning was a swamp of muck and slime later became a nursery farm occupied by an abundance of beautiful shrubs, flowers, and plant life. It began to grow in scope and size and eventually embraced several thousand acres of land in Norfolk County. It was the largest nursery farm in the South and one of the largest in the entire nation. More than 5,000 varieties of plant life, ranging from the hardy oak to the delicate camellia, were grown there. There were numerous hot houses for more fragile plants. The constant experimentation that was carried on at the nursery resulted in newer and sometimes more hardy plants and trees. Each group of plants was catalogued, making it easier to locate a particular one when needed. Greenbrier served the local customer as well as customers throughout the world. Although a large amount of the land has been sold, Greenbrier Farms still exist today.

In the 1970s, most of the land that had once been the world's largest nursery was sold and Greenbrier Parkway was built. Even today when driving along the parkway, one can still see magnolias and other trees that were a part of Greenbrier Farms and Nursery. Around 1981, land was acquired on Greenbrier Parkway and the citizens of Chesapeake received their own local mall. Many truckloads of dirt were hauled in to create a huge mound on which Greenbrier Mall was built—thus, the main entrance places the customer on the second level instead of the first.

One of the longtime tenants of the mall is Waldenbooks. Though not generally known by the many patrons of the store, this establishment has its own ghost, which has shown himself to several employees. It is not known if this spirit, which stands 6 feet in height and appears in a white robe, frequents the other stores or shops or if he is just interested in reading. It seems that he has nothing better to do than glide through the store, pull books off the shelves, and laugh as they hit the floor. If you are a lover of books, you just might meet him sometime.

The planned community of Greenbrier is home to many Chesapeake residents. It also has a large number of restaurants, other shopping centers, and stores of many kinds and sizes.

When the city turned 20 years old, a decision was made to celebrate, and it was in May 1983 that the first Chesapeake Jubilee was held. At that time, the City did not have a suitable place to hold the event, so it was held in and around the Greenbrier Mall. The midway around the mall was the site of 50 game and food booths as well as various displays and activities. The first jubilee began on Thursday, May 13, 1983, at 3:30 p.m. and closed on Sunday, May 15, 1983, at 7:00 p.m. Former Mayor Marian Whitehurst was general chairperson of the first jubilee task force.

In November 1985, the City of Chesapeake purchased 70 acres of land near the correctional unit on Greenbrier Parkway. It was not officially designated as the jubilee site but was generally understood that it would be developed for that and several other purposes. The final cost was $857, 500, with interest-free payments spread over a ten-year period. The site was ready when the jubilee was held May 16, 17, and 18, 1986. The jubilee for the year 2001 was held on May 18, 19, and 20.

The places of interest and available activities in the city are almost endless. There are approximately 50 parks and recreation centers, and the YMCA has two locations in Chesapeake. The Chesapeake Arboretum has been said to be one of the best-kept secrets in the city. It offers walking trails that take one through a forest containing many different kinds of trees and gardens; it is also known for its antique rose gardens. The arboretum's headquarters at 624 Oak Grove Road is located in a farmhouse that dates back to 1730.

Northwest is located in the southern part of Chesapeake near the dividing line between Virginia and North Carolina. The park, which offers boating, fishing, hiking, campsites, and other forms of outdoor recreation, contains more than 700 acres and can be reached from Indian Creek Road. The cypress trees and stumps are responsible for the color of the river water at Northwest. A few years ago, no one would have believed that one day 85 percent of the water used in the City of Chesapeake would come from the Northwest River. A water treatment plant was built, but the water contained a high percentage of salt from the Albemarle Sound in North Carolina. In 1998, the quality of drinking water was improved by a process called reverse osmosis.

In 1979, Chesapeake was the only city in Hampton Roads without a YMCA building. The building grew out of a discussion among a small group of city leaders. School Superintendent Fred Bateman was chairman of the Y's management committee. It took six years, but on July 29, 1985, the Chesapeake YMCA opened its doors to more than 2,000 charter members. Mayor J. Bennie Jennings Jr. presided over the formal dedication, which took place the third week of August 1985.

Gary D. Graham, general executive of the YMCA of Tidewater, presented a plaque that listed the names of major contributors. He also presented a special plaque honoring the family of Warren L. Aleck, a member of the management committee and chief operating officer of Earl's Markets. Aleck spearheaded the fund-raising campaign to build the facility, and his family donated most of the money needed to construct the swimming pool. The building, which contained 17,732 square feet, was constructed at 1033 Greenbrier Parkway. Throughout the years, several additions have been made to the original structure. In the early 1990s, the building on Old Greenbrier Road, which had previously been occupied by the Ace of Clubs racquetball club, became available, and a second YMCA was opened at that location.

CHESAPEAKE'S MUSEUM AND INFORMATION CENTER

The history behind Chesapeake's Museum and Information Center began more than 100 years ago, when on August 31, 1895, School District Number Five of Norfolk County acquired a parcel of land in Washington Magisterial District from the Shea family. The land was situated on the east side of the public road, which had formerly been known as the Berkley and Currituck Turnpike. The road was 40 feet wide. It is interesting to note the descriptive location of the stakes placed by the surveyors. One was in the branch near a spring on the roadside, another in the center of a cove, and reference was made to the lines of the lands of B.F. Gibson and A.A. Spain. The deed stated that the piece of land "contained an acre, less a small fraction of an acre and the school district would have the right to use the spring on the roadside, located near the northwest corner of the land." This property on which a new four-room brick school was built in 1908 was purchased for the sum of $150.

A pre-construction notice for the building was found in the July 16, 1908 edition of a building journal called the *Manufacturers' Record*. It stated, "Portlock, Va.-Bids will be opened July 22 for erection of four-room brick school building at Portlock; certified check, $500; plans and specifications on file at office of Ferguson & Calrow, architects, Norfolk, Va., or at office of A.H. Foreman, Superintendent of Public Schools Norfolk County, Chamberlaine Building, Norfolk, Va." John W. Jones, a local contractor, built the school.

The neighborhood where the school was constructed was called Raleigh Heights, and according to fire insurance maps, the building was known as the Portlock Public School No. 5. Schools of the period were usually heated by wood or coal, which was burned in old potbellied stoves. Also, the ceilings were 12 or 13 feet in height and each room in the school was equipped with a large

These older students pose on the front steps of the Portlock School on Bainbridge Boulevard a few years after it opened in 1908. By the time this photograph was taken, a concrete sidewalk had replaced the old wooden boardwalk in front of the school.

cloakroom. It is not certain if the school building was initially wired for electricity or if it was equipped with a furnace. In those days, natural lighting was relied on and it was typical for schools to have large windows on at least two walls of each classroom. One thing it did not have was indoor plumbing. There was a frame outbuilding to the rear of the school that was connected to the main building by a wooden platform. One side of the outhouse was for the boys and the other side was for the girls.

Drawings of the building on the Sanborn Fire Insurance map of 1928 indicated that the building had electricity and a furnace. A larger building called the Portlock High School was also shown on the map. It was located east of the Portlock Public School No. 5. The insurance map of 1950 shows School No. 5, the high school, a gymnasium just east of the high school, and another building designated as the Portlock Public School, which was across the street and north of the high school. It was labeled as having been built in 1944.

Apparently some time in the earlier years, the ceilings of School No. 5 were lowered. Information concerning plans for restoration of the building indicated that the lowered ceilings would be removed.

When the school was erected in 1908, members of the Board of Trustees of the Washington District of Norfolk County included E.M. Tilley (chairman), M.C. Keeling (clerk), and T.W. Butt. In the early years, the school served not only the students of Portlock but also those from the surrounding sections of Norfolk County between South Norfolk and Oak Grove. After the building was no longer used as a school, it served as administrative offices for the school system and later was used by the Jaycees. Eventually, Portlock School No. 5 was boarded up and was awaiting demolition when a group of concerned citizens intervened.

On September 18, 1990, the Chesapeake Historic Preservation Steering Committee sent a letter to members of the Chesapeake City Council expressing their support and requesting that the council consider renovation of the old Portlock School building for possible use as a museum and information center. The committee also recommended the creation of a foundation to administer fund-raising and oversee the renovation and management of the building.

More than a year had passed, when on January 21, 1992, approximately 25 citizens appeared before the city council in support of preserving and renovating the Portlock School. These citizens represented a number of organizations within the city. An editorial, which appeared in the *Chesapeake Clipper* on January 28, 1992, described the 84-year-old school as a handsome, columned brick building on Bainbridge Boulevard in South Norfolk. At that time, it was empty and boarded up.

The citizens envisioned the schoolhouse as a repository for history and art. It was said that it could house artifacts from the area's 360 years of history, and the walls could be filled with the works of local artists. A civic chorus had dreams in which they could hear the voices of its members, while another group pictured young dancers gliding across the wooden floors. The local historical society had hoped that the city would some day have a museum. The Chesapeake Fine Arts Commission, the Chesapeake Civic Chorus, and the Chesapeake Community Theater had for a long time lobbied for a fine arts center. But then as now, economic conditions were such that there was no money for what were considered luxuries. In the earlier years of the city, the old saying was "The only culture in Chesapeake is agriculture."

In late February 1992, City Manager James W. Rein adjusted his proposed construction budget so that the old Portlock School could be transformed into a cultural center. He had included $340,000 to be used toward the arts. This money was to be spent in the 1992–1993 fiscal year for asbestos removal and to bring the building up to code. When the city council met in work session, some of the members were against the project; however, it was decided that even if the building was demolished, the asbestos would have to be removed. After much ado, the $340,000 was added to the capital improvement budget.

The initial group meeting was held on March 12, 1992, in the City Clerk's Conference Room. Those present were the mayor, city manager, city council liaison, intergovernmental affairs, and staff members of the Parks and Recreation Department. Representatives from the historical society, South Norfolk Civic League, Council of Churches, and Fine Arts Commission were also present. The main topics of discussion were possible uses for the building, the historical preservation designation process, and the need for architectural review and formation of a non-profit organization to oversee the use and renovation process. It was at this time that the name of "Chesapeake Consortium for the Arts" was given to the group. Members of the consortium, city staff, and councilpersons met on March 27, 1992, to further discuss these subjects. The entire group toured the old school building, noting the layout as four rooms with a center hallway.

The next meeting of the group was held on April 16, 1992, at the South Norfolk Community Center. A permanent chairman was appointed, and members were asked to serve on various committees dealing with such issues as by-laws, marketing, program, finance, building renovation, and preservation. When the consortium met on May 21, 1992, it was determined that the regular meetings would be held at 11:00 a.m. on the second Thursday of each month at the South Norfolk Community Center.

About that time, lead was discovered throughout the building and was included in the contract for removal of asbestos. The group continued to meet monthly; by-laws and articles of incorporation were written and approved. Application was made with the Internal Revenue Service for 501(3)(c) designation. On September 10, 1992, the name was changed again—this time the group approved the name of "Chesapeake Consortium for Arts & History." The bid process for removal of asbestos and lead did not start until late September or early October 1992. In October 1992, the members were informed that a board of directors consisting of a minimum of three persons was required to be in place before the incorporation process could be completed. On December 10, 1992, the renovation committee reported that a low bid to remove the lead and asbestos had been received from Coleman Construction, and the item would be on the city council agenda for December 15, 1992. The council voted to accept the bid and awarded the contract

Recess was over for the day on May 6, 1955, as students line up to go back inside the Portlock School. This back entrance, with considerable changes, is used today by museum patrons.

for removal to Coleman. The contractor agreed to start work on or about January 24, 1993.

When the consortium met on February 11, 1993, they discussed a permanent dues structure and agreed that one would be in place by July 1, 1993. Plans were also made for the first annual meeting to be held on April 8, 1993, at 7:00 p.m. in the South Norfolk Community Center.

On February 23, 1993, a group of interested citizens approached the Chesapeake City Council and requested more information on the proposed use of the building. The following day, the board of directors of the consortium met to discuss the issues raised at the city council the night before and agreed to a meeting with those citizens in order to alleviate any concerns. Those citizens and all other interested parties were invited to attend the next general meeting, to be held on March 11, 1993, at the South Norfolk Community Center.

There were conflicts among the consortium members as to what the building should be used for. The organization had a 35-member board of directors, and members were trying to raise funds, but did not know what the money would be used for. The first president resigned due to what he called "constant disagreement and politicizing."

One group wanted to remove the partition between the rooms and install a stage. This would have destroyed the chances of the building being placed on the National Historic Register. A letter received from an architectural historian stated that the building would serve its function as a school museum best if the historic

John Jones built the old Portlock School in 1908 on what had formerly been known as the Berkley and Currituck Turnpike. Chesapeake's Museum now occupies the building.

classroom spaces were preserved in their original configuration. He also stated that the preferred priority for historic rehabilitation projects is to keep and repair the historic materials wherever possible.

In May 1993, a meeting was held at the South Norfolk Community Center. Three council members, Assistant City Manager Clarence Cuffee, and many citizens attended it. Cuffee presided over the meeting and was pleased with the outcome. On May 25, 1993, the city council gave its approval and agreed to turn the Portlock School into a museum and information center.

After removal of the asbestos and lead was completed, the windows were replaced. The inside of the building was gutted to its brick walls and only the wooden skeletons of the four classrooms and coat closets remained. The structure was solid but a moderate amount of the flooring had to be replaced. All the usable flooring was salvaged and used in two of the rooms and the halls. Two rooms received new wooden floors, which were covered with carpet. Three restrooms and a small kitchen were added in the building. The cloakroom in the front classroom on the northeast corner of the building was turned into a gift shop. During the renovation process, several tons of coal and some slate blackboards were found in the basement.

The City of Chesapeake Parks and Recreation Department oversaw renovation of the building. The architectural firm of Hanbury, Evans, Newill, Vlattas and Company was hired by the City. The structural engineers on the project were McPherson and Associates, and the mechanical and electrical engineers were Hickman and Ambrose. The firm of Langley and McDonald performed civil engineering and landscaping duties, and the general contractor was Spencer Building Corporation.

On October 2, 1995, members of the board of directors met with representatives of Chesapeake Parks and Recreation Department and Vice Mayor Nance to review the 65 percent blueprints of the museum. At that time, it had been determined that work would begin in April 1996 and would be completed in nine months. There were delays in design and other phases of the restoration process that amounted to approximately six months.

In mid-1996, leaders from the City announced that when the fire department vacated the garage next door, the building would be made available for use by the museum. Renovation of the garage began in early 1997 and was completed around the end of June of the same year.

Early efforts at fund-raising included a successful dinner, which was held at the Moose Lodge in Portsmouth. A profit of around $1,650 was realized. A mailing requesting donations was not beneficial. Thanks to the efforts of Senator Mark Early and Delegate Lionel Spruill, the museum received a grant of $100,000 from the State Legislature. Those funds became available on July 1, 1996, through the Department of Historical Resources. The next money received by the museum was the sum of $207.90 from Ms. Gale Harris's sixth- and seventh-grade classes at Great Bridge Middle School. The classes, which were receiving instructions in the stock market, formed their own company, made "pun nuts," and sold them.

The organization had T-shirts made with the museum logo on the front. These were sold for $12.50 each. On Monday, February 24, 1997, Senator Early spoke at a dinner given by the South Norfolk Woman's Club; in his speech, he announced that the State Legislature had appropriated another $100,000 for use by the museum and that this money would become available on July 1, 1997. When the Chesapeake City Council met on Tuesday, May 13, 1997, the members voted unanimously to grant $12,500 to help pay the museum director's salary for the first year of operation.

After the interior of the building was completed, a concerted effort was applied to the grounds and parking lot. Shrubbery was planted, sod was placed in the areas of drainage, grass seed was sown, and antique pole lamps were installed around the building and parking lot. On April 8, 1997, power was applied to the lamps, which were set to come on at dusk and cut-off at daylight. The lamps produce a picturesque scene at 3815 Bainbridge Boulevard.

The official dedication ceremony was held on Wednesday, May 21, 1997, at 11:00 a.m. Mayor William E. Ward spoke, as did Claire Askew, director of the City of Chesapeake Parks and Recreation. Dr. Raymond Jones talked about his days as a student at the old school. Mayor Ward then presented the key to Pauline Dennis, president of the board.

After the dedication, director Ruth Akright (she had been hired April 1, 1997), began the job of creating a museum and information center. Office equipment and supplies had to be purchased, display cases built, and the gift shop set up. Once the display cases were in place, they had to be filled with artifacts. The job was accomplished and the museum was opened with a reception for the general public in February 1998.

The museum received its third grant of $100,000 from the State Legislature, effective July 1, 2000. This grant, like the other two, had to be matched dollar for dollar. The match was accomplished by donations of money or artifacts and volunteer hours.

Chesapeake's Museum and Information Center has had its share of ups and downs, in-fighting, and bad press, some truthful and some not. Finally, all is quiet on the "Chesapeake front," and there are many things of interest for the citizens of Chesapeake to see and learn. On December 1, 1993, there were 72 members. Those 72 are considered to be charter members. Several of them have passed away, and many others have just disappeared. The museum has had four presidents since it was organized. The first president was John Ben Gibson Jr.; the first vice president was Pauline Dennis. Other presidents have included Pauline Dennis, Roland Thornton, and Raymond Harper (through the year 2002).

Captain Frederic E. Consolvo Jr. Armory

Many male citizens of the old City of South Norfolk were members of the National Guard and were activated early in World War II. After the war, South Norfolk still had a large population of National Guard members, but did not have

The formal dedication of the Captain Frederic E. Consolvo Jr. Armory took place on May 12, 1956. The daylong festivities began at 11:00 a.m. with a parade of national guardsmen marching past the Grand Theatre on Chesapeake Avenue in South Norfolk.

an armory where they could meet. Colonel Clarence Forehand's individual campaign to bring an armory to the City of South Norfolk began as early as 1948, when as mayor of the city, he began quietly writing letters pointing out the city's needs for such a building. Forehand stated that Louis A. Oliver, a Norfolk architect, made drawings for the structure in 1949. This was done in anticipation of a state allocation for the unit. He pointed out that the city desperately needed an armory for its reserve units. Forehand told the council that he could safely refer to the structure as a civic center, since armories were often used for that purpose. He gave as an example the City of Richmond, which received money into its treasury from use of its armory. In 1952, Forehand and others carried a request to the State Legislature. In June 1954, the city council passed a resolution endorsing the armory and requested funds from the state and federal governments.

In early 1954, the city fathers in anticipation of building a civic center purchased a plat of land, 5.5 acres in all. The site, which was originally known as the Marcellus George estate, is on the South Norfolk Basin and is a peninsula bounded on the north by Bainbridge Boulevard and to the east of Williams Avenue. In September, the City of South Norfolk negotiated with the American Oil Company to swap this property plus $20,000 for a 5-acre site on Bainbridge Boulevard. Louis W. Ballou, of the architectural firm, endorsed the move to the new site in December 1954. He termed it a more desirable location for an armory.

Forehand, Mayor N.J. Babb, acting City Manager Philip P. Davis, and other officials attended the ground breaking, which took place in early November 1955.

Construction was under the supervision of James T. Corson of the Southern Engineering and Construction Company of Richmond, Virginia. Ballou and Justice, a firm of architects and engineers of Richmond, accomplished the architectural work. The building permit stated that the project was set up on a 180-day completion schedule.

The building was one of three new armories built in the state that year in connection with a National Guard expansion program.

The structure fronts on Bainbridge Boulevard between Barnes and Williams Roads (now Lester Street) and measures about 125 by 184 feet—its long side flanking Williams Road. The interior plans called for a large assembly area with provisions for a high school–size basketball court, a classroom measuring 22 by 20 feet, a large kitchen, and an arrangement of toilets, store rooms, and locker facilities. The assembly area could accommodate about 400 telescoping bleacher seats or about 700 conventional chairs. The building was designed to serve as an armory and a civic gathering place for the community. The cost was $250,000 with the City's share being $43,500.

In early March 1956, the South Norfolk City Council passed a resolution naming the new armory in memory of Captain Frederic E. Consolvo Jr., who enlisted in the National Guard in 1932. He was a second lieutenant when the 29th Division was activated in 1941. The formal dedication took place on May 12, 1956; the dedicatory address was delivered by Representative Porter Hardy Jr.

Both military and civilian officials from neighboring communities, the state, and nation flanked Representative Hardy. Governor Thomas B. Stanley was expected to attend, but had to decline because of other engagements.

Colonel Clarence Forehand addressed dignitaries and citizens in front of the armory during the dedication ceremony in May 1956.

Captain Frederic E. Consolvo Jr., after whom Chesapeake's armory on Bainbridge Boulevard is named, was killed in France on August 25, 1944.

The daylong festivities began at 11:00 a.m. with an all-military parade. A luncheon for more than 1,000 guests followed the dedication. An open house was held in the afternoon and early evening, and the night activities included a formal military ball. The dedication was under the direction of official committees from the National Guard and the City of South Norfolk.

The city committee was made up of Mayor Babb, Councilman Linwood L. Briggs Jr., City Manager Earnest L. Thacker, Police Chief W.E. Beedie, and Fire Prevention Bureau Chief Ove Yensen. William J. Story, school superintendent for South Norfolk, served as the master of ceremonies, and Chief Yensen was the parade marshall.

Fred Consolvo was a Boy Scout, an altar boy at St. Brides Episcopal Church, a proud member of the South Norfolk High School football team, and a real gentleman. After graduation from high school, he was accepted into the apprentice program at the Norfolk Naval Shipyard in Portsmouth, Virginia, and graduated in 1941, the same year that the United States entered World War II. Consolvo had been plagued by poor eyesight most of his life; with this, along with the facts that he had a wife, two young children, and held a defense job, he very well could have avoided going into active duty with the other members of the 29th Division. But, he felt it was his duty to fight for his country and his beliefs.

135

Fred and his brother Bill, an Army paratrooper, were among the thousands of men who invaded France on D-Day. Their parents received a letter from Captain Consolvo on August 23, 1944, and it was to be his last letter, for he was killed in action on August 25, 1944. In this letter, dated July 1944, he described war as a dirty, miserable sore that eats out the soul of humanity. The only information that the family ever received was that he was killed on the front lines during a battle in France. Frederic Consolvo was buried in the 29th Army Division Cemetery in France.

In 1982, the City of Chesapeake withdrew support for the armory and the State assumed the $33,000 operating cost. Restructuring and budget cuts by the Department of Defense forced closure of the armory in 1995. In 1996, the State turned the site over to the City of Chesapeake. At that time, the building was not boarded up, and as a result, it was vandalized, abandoned, and neglected. The plumbing, copper wiring, and all fixtures were stolen and most likely were sold at a local junkyard for a large amount of money. After the "horse was out of the barn," all the windows and doors were secured with plywood.

After the armory was vacated, the City received several bids by companies that wanted to buy the building and 5 acres for bargain prices. South Norfolk Civic leaders decided to ask the City to turn the armory over to them for renovation, after which it would be returned to the City of Chesapeake. Once renovated, the building could be used as a multi-purpose center, which would house offices and serve senior citizens and the youth of the community. It could also be used by the City to replace spaces now being rented by some of its departments. The initial estimate to renovate the armory was about $250,000; that cost has escalated and will continue to do so with each passing year until completion.

CHESAPEAKE PUBLIC SCHOOLS

As previously stated, there was no Chesapeake, Virginia, before 1963, and after the merger, a lot of intelligent educators joined forces and formed the Chesapeake Public School system. Previously, the City of South Norfolk and Norfolk County each had their own system of public education.

Virginians have been interested in education since early in the seventeenth century. Many of the first citizens of Norfolk County had been educated in England, but in the colonies, it was difficult to provide an education for their children. Large distances separated families, and travel was mostly by boat, making it almost impossible to establish schools that could serve all the children.

Because of the obstacles involved, education became a family responsibility. The typical school of colonial Virginia was conducted by a member of the clergy or by a private tutor hired by a planter. The pupils at those schools were the planter's children and sometimes the children of his nearest white neighbors.

To understand early education in Virginia, one has to go back to 1796, when Thomas Jefferson introduced his plan for the "General Diffusion of Knowledge." It was through his influence and suggestion that on December 22,

1796, that the General Assembly of Virginia enacted a school law entitled "An Act to Establish Schools."

Two years later, Norfolk County adopted Jefferson's plan and put into operation a system of public education. The county's colonial leaders accepted this point of view, and it has served as a guide during the years that have followed for citizens of Norfolk County and for those of that area of the county that in 1919 became the town of South Norfolk.

In 1799, schools were opened in several areas of Norfolk County for the free instruction of children for a period of three years. One of the schools was located at Hickory Ground, a community in the southeast section of the county along the Great Road, on which was the "Great Bridge," where one of the first battles of the Revolutionary War was fought and won by the Virginians. This later became an academy for primary, grammar, and high school studies. In 1835, the old frame or log cabin was replaced by a brick structure, incorporated by the General Assembly, and given the name of St. Brides Academy. Another school was located in the northwest section of the county in the community later known as Churchland. In 1802, it became known as the Craney Island School, and in 1840, when it was rebuilt, the institution was known as the Sycamore Hill School. It was rebuilt again in 1854. In 1872, the Norfolk County Court incorporated one branch of this school under the name of the Churchland Academy.

In 1845, Norfolk County put into operation a complete system of public schools for the benefit of all free white children of the county. By authority of the

At the age of 16, Miss Rena B. Wright became governess to the Hyslop children in Brambleton and later was tutor to the daughters of Dr. N.G. Wilson of Norfolk County. She taught and served as assistant and principal of area schools for more than 45 years. Wright retired from the South Norfolk school system in June 1942. A few years later the elementary school was named for her. This photograph appeared in the 1925 yearbook.

General Assembly, enacted February 17, 1845, a board of school commissioners met at Deep Creek. They organized and elected Leroy G. Edwards (chairman), George T. Wallace (clerk), and Stephen B. Tatem (treasurer). The commissioners arranged for the opening of 20 schools with 3 local trustees for each school. The trustees were instructed to provide a building and employ a teacher for a term of 10 months at a salary of $30 per month, to be paid out of public funds.

At a meeting of the county commissioners in June 1849, the Reverend Thomas Hume was elected the first superintendent of schools for Norfolk County with a salary of $500 per annum. He served for two years and was succeeded by Leroy G. Edwards, who had been chairman of the board of commissioners for seven years. He served as superintendent for 10 years. Between 1845 and 1861, the number of schools grew to 30.

The superb system of 30 schools, which had been open 10 months per year for 16 years and had accomplished so much for the county, came suddenly to an end. In the spring of 1862, the Federal army took possession of the cities and the county of Norfolk. The schools were closed and the buildings destroyed. Some were burned, while others were torn down by U.S. soldiers and the timbers were moved to military camps and used to build winter quarters for the troops. Among the schools destroyed were those at Wallaceton, Cornland, Good Hope, Bell's Mill, and Tanner's Creek.

The constitution of 1869, the fourth of Virginia's six constitutions, was adopted by the state convention, which met at Richmond from December 3, 1867 to April 17, 1868. The constitution was ratified by popular vote on July 6, 1869, and

H.C. Mann took this early photograph of the Oakwood School in the Pleasant Grove area of Chesapeake. Between 1907 and 1923, Mann took many pictures of scenes throughout Hampton Roads.

among other things, provided for the establishment of Virginia's first statewide system of public schools. Governor Gilbert C. Walker commissioned Captain John T. "Tom" West as superintendent of schools for Norfolk County. Captain West wrote in his journal that he "received notice of my appointment to the office Co. Supt. of schools in December 1869 and entered upon the discharge of duties of the office January 1, 1870." His instructions were to recommend to the State Board of Education three suitable men from each magisterial district of the county to form a county school board. The six districts included Western Branch, Deep Creek, Pleasant Grove, Butts Road, Washington, and Tanner's Creek.

On January 20, 1871, the trustees met at the Norfolk County Courthouse in Portsmouth and organized the Norfolk County School Board with superintendent John T. West, ex-officio chairman, and Captain Thomas M. Hodges, clerk. After hearing a report from Superintendent West as to the powers of the board and the deplorable condition of education in the county, the board instructed the district trustees to by resolution request the board of supervisors of the county to submit the question of levying a tax of 30¢ on each $100 of real and personal property to the vote of the people at the forthcoming May election. The tax was to be used to form a district and county fund to supplement that of the state. This assured moderate support for the 30 schools that had opened on April 1, 1870.

Superintendent West served three terms. In 1882, he was succeeded by Jesse E. Baker, who served four years, after which Captain West was again elected to the position and served until 1908. He was then replaced by A.H. Foreman. West had served the Norfolk County schools for approximately 35 years.

The schools of Norfolk County continued to progress, and the establishment of high schools began to receive support from its citizens. In 1906, plans were made for a high school to be located in the small village of South Norfolk. The following year, one was erected in the Great Bridge area.

By 1907, there were 168 schools with an enrollment of 8,400 children. The average school year was nine months, and teacher salaries had improved, with the maximum being $110 per month. When the 1916 school year began, there were seven high schools in Norfolk County, and six were accredited.

World Wars I and II brought an influx of residents, and there was a dramatic increase in school enrollment; however, some new residents returned to their hometowns at the end of both wars. From 1940 to 1947, school enrollment tripled, and the anticipated decrease in the number of schoolchildren after World War II did not occur. In 1946, the transition from an 11- to 12-year school system began to take place, and this added to the existing problem of overcrowded schools. New school buildings were needed, and in 1950, a $4-million bond referendum received a favorable vote from the citizens of Norfolk County. The school population continued to rise, and in 1960, another bond program for $6 million was approved for school requirements.

On January 1, 1963, Norfolk County ceased to exist. It was on that date that the City of South Norfolk and Norfolk County merged to form the City of

Chesapeake. The school boards combined, with E.W. Chittum becoming the first superintendent of Chesapeake Public Schools. He remained in the position until 1975.

One of the first new learning tools acquired by the Chesapeake School System was a planetarium. In June 1963, Chesapeake became the first public school system in Virginia to have its own. Under its 30-foot dome, thousands of stars and planets can be simulated, as well as solar and lunar eclipses and the motions of the sun, moon, and planets.

New schools were built throughout Chesapeake, including Indian River and Western Branch High Schools. Later, new high schools for Deep Creek, Great Bridge, and a new Oscar Smith and Hickory High were built. Oscar Smith became very wealthy in the local fertilizer business but died in his early 1950s after falling off a horse. His wife offered to donate $50,000 for a new school if the school's stadium would be named after Smith. The city council voted to name both the stadium and the school after him. Today there are two schools in Chesapeake that bear his name.

New elementary schools would come up in Portlock, Greenbrier, Great Bridge, and Western Branch. New middle schools were completed in Deep Creek and Hickory. Dedication ceremonies for the Hugo A. Owens and Hickory Middle Schools were held on Sunday, March 29, 1998. New and larger schools, ranging from $40 to 50 million each, are continuously being built—the $35,000 or even the $1 million school is a thing of the past.

The following are the superintendents of Norfolk County/Chesapeake schools:

Reverend Thomas Hume	1849–1851
Leroy G. Edwards	1852–1862
John T. West	1870–1881
Jesse E. Baker	1882–1885
John T. West	1886–1908
A.H. Foreman	1908–1916
James Hunt	1917–1942
Henry I. Willett Sr.	1942–1945
William A. Early	1946–1948
Edwin W. Chittum	1949–1975
Kenneth Fulp	1976–1980
C. Fred Bateman	1981–1995
W. Randolph Nichols	1995 to present

CHESAPEAKE PUBLIC SERVICE

Public safety for all citizens began when the first legislative body in America met in a small church at Jamestown one hour before sunrise on July 30, 1619. The meeting, which was called to order by Governor George Yeardley, consisted of members of his council, the Reverend Richard Buck, and representatives of the two precincts in existence at that time.

Prior to the year 1634, Virginia had no uniform county system or organization. By that time, the spread of the plantations away from Jamestown made it necessary to institute a system of local government. It was then that the colony was divided into eight shires or counties. Each of these counties had its own court of records presided over by a bench of justices who were known as "County Commissioners." Each county had a sheriff and a clerk of the court. In 1634, the bounds of Elizabeth City County included what would become Norfolk and Princess Anne Counties and also a part of Nansemond. It is believed that a new county known as "New Norfolk" was formed in 1636 from land extending south of the James River and Hampton Roads. It is certain that two counties were organized in 1637, one was known as "Upper Norfolk" and included the bounds of Nansemond County. The other formed was given the name "Lower Norfolk County."

Adam Thoroughgood convinced the General Assembly to create a new county, and as a result, he was appointed presiding justice over the court. Thoroughgood was born in 1604 and was the seventh son of an English vicar. He arrived in Virginia in 1621 as an indentured servant of Edward Waters. He completed his indenture in 1625 and received his first land grant the same year. Two years later, Thoroughgood returned to England and married Sarah Offley, daughter of a wealthy London merchant. Adam and Sarah left England and took up residence in Virginia.

The first recorded court session in the new county was held at Adam Thoroughgood's house at Lynnhaven on May 15, 1637. Two cases were tried that

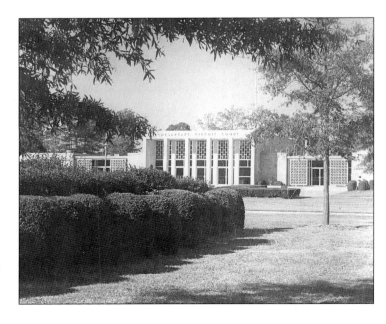

This was the location of the Chesapeake Circuit Court until 1999. At that time a new court building was completed and the circuit court moved. This structure has since been demolished.

141

first day. The first was that of Anne Fowler, who was accused of saying insulting words against, of all people, Adam Thoroughgood. She was found guilty, received 20 lashes, and was required to attend the next service at the parish church to publicly confess her sin and apologize to Thoroughgood. The second case was that involving Bartholomew Haynes and Julia Underwood—"she being bigg with child." The punishment was a wedding between the two young people.

Sessions of the county court continued to be held monthly at various private homes. Usually the homes were located near rivers or creeks, as most travel in those days was by water.

The first trial by jury held in Lower Norfolk County was between Richard Foster and John Gookin. Gookin's hogs got into Foster's cornfield and destroyed his crop. The jury returned a verdict in favor of Gookin because he had a hog pen and Foster's field was not fenced in.

In March 1654, the General Assembly authorized the county to create a port in each parish. The port or market place was to contain a court, church, tavern, ordinary, and a variety of shops. By this time Lower Norfolk County had been divided into two parishes. A decision was made to establish one marketplace on the Elizabeth River on the land of William Shipp and another on the Lynnhaven River on land belonging to Adam Thoroughgood's widow and descendants. Before construction could begin, the legislation authorizing the marketplaces was cancelled by the General Assembly. In January 1660, the justices decided to build a single courthouse on land acquired from Thomas Hardy. This piece of property was on Broad Creek.

While the courthouse was under construction, Thomas Hardy allowed the justices to hold court in his home. The courthouse was completed in the latter part of 1661. On September 17, 1689, members of the court reported that the structure on Broad Creek was in ruins and beyond repair. A decision was made to build two courthouses in the county. One was to be built on the Elizabeth River near Norfolk Towne and the other on land belonging to Edward Cooper on the Lynnhaven River. Sessions were to be held in August, December, and February at Lynnhaven and in the other months, at the Towne of Norfolk. This was to make the court available to all citizens.

In 1691, Lower Norfolk County was divided into Norfolk and Princess Anne Counties. In the summer, work was begun on a new courthouse in Norfolk, and it was completed in 1694. In 1789, the legislature chose Powder Point as the location for the next Norfolk County courthouse. In 1801, the county courthouse was moved to Portsmouth, where it remained until 1963, when the City of Chesapeake was formed.

The records that were preserved in the office of the Norfolk County clerk in Portsmouth are now in the office of the clerk of the Circuit Court of the City of Chesapeake. Those records began on May 15, 1637, and have with few exceptions, been kept up to the present time.

Before the merger between the City of South Norfolk and Norfolk County, the Norfolk County Board of Supervisors met monthly at the courthouse in

Portsmouth. Before South Norfolk became a town in 1919, it had a supervisor that represented the village at each meeting. After becoming a township, South Norfolk's government consisted of a mayor, nine councilmen, treasurer, clerk of the common council, and the town sergeant.

Throughout the years, hundreds of dollars have been appropriated by a variety of organization to be used for restoration of old Norfolk County records. Among the contributors were the Norfolk County Board of Supervisors, the Norfolk-Tidewater Committee of Colonial Dames, the Fort Nelson Chapter, National Society Daughters of the American Revolution, and others.

CHESAPEAKE POLICE

The office of sheriff came into being around 1634, when the colony was divided into eight counties. A list of those who served in the position will most likely never be complete, for some served only a few months.

Some of the men who held the position are listed below along with the year in which they first took office:

Captain Sibsey	1645
Richard Conquest	1649
Captain William Carver	1672
Anthony Lawson	1682
Anthony Lawson	1685
Samuel Boush	1722
Colonel George Newton	1728
Samuel Smith	1740
William Portlock	1741
William Ivey	1752
Robert Tucker	1755
Charles Sweny	1757
Thomas Veale	1776
William Booker	1785
James Williams	1812
Arthur Butt	1819
Mordecai Cooke	1832
Holt Wilson	1835
John M. Drewry	1854
Samuel E. Etheridge	1868
John Lesner	1878
A.C. Cromwell	1900
A.A. Wendell	1920
Arthur Hodges	1944
John R. Newhart	1969 to present

Sheriff A.A. Wendell and members of the Norfolk County Police Department stand beside their cars outside the armory on Elm Avenue in 1941.

Prior to September 1919, South Norfolk was a flourishing community in the Washington Magisterial District of Norfolk County. As such, police protection was afforded to the village by members of the Norfolk County Police Department; however, an article in the Norfolk newspaper, which reported a shooting on Saturday night, January 11, 1913, stated the following:

> Joseph Spence was shot in the hip by Lum Going. Domestic troubles are said to have been at the bottom of the affray. The man who did the shooting was arrested by Chief of Police E.H. Whitehurst of South Norfolk and lodged in the county jail. His trial was fixed at the jail this afternoon at 4 o'clock by Magistrate J.T. Smith.

Was this a misprint? According to records, South Norfolk did not have a police force until around 1920.

Members of the South Norfolk Police Department, *c.* 1921, were Chief Paul "Polly" Warden, Clayton C. Ansell, Will Harris, Vernon Spruill, Bill Horton, and motorcycle officer Sergeant Sam Duvall.

After Chief Warden resigned, the South Norfolk Police Department was supervised by a police board, which was composed of patrolmen and civilians. The board governed until 1935, when E.L. "Ed" Boyce assumed the position as chief of police. Others that served as chief are as follows: Henry L. Scheuerman, beginning in 1944; J.K. Holland Jr., 1948; William E. Beedie Jr., 1952; Donald Leet, 1956; Allen L. "Junie" Ford Jr., 1957; and R.C. Hardy, 1958.

On Thursday, October 18, 1962, it was announced in the *Virginian-Pilot* that Captain Wilbur E. Sears of the Norfolk County Police Department would become chief of police of the new city. The following men have served as police chief for the City of Chesapeake: Wilbur E. Sears, beginning in 1963; Albion B. Roane Jr., 1969; Roland A. Lakoski, 1971; Ian M. Shipley Jr., 1990; Richard A. Justice, 1996 to present.

The public safety officer was introduced in Chesapeake in 1969, when A.B. Roane was chief of police. This was a concept whereby officers were trained in both police and fire science. Before this, the police and fire services were completely separate. The public safety concept, which had been introduced on an experimental basis, became a reality as all uniformed officers within the police division became public safety officers and began training in the science of firefighting.

As the City of Chesapeake began to grow in leaps and bounds, it became necessary to build more and larger buildings to house the city's operations. On January 10, 1987, the ground-breaking ceremony for the new city hall was held. James Rein was city manager, and Sidney M. Oman was mayor. The dedication was held on January 14, 1989, and James Rein was still city manager, but the

Pictured here are two early motorcycle officers of the Chesapeake Police Department. They are John Newhart, left, and George Paspas, right.

mayor was now David I. Wynne. Members of the city council had appointed all previous mayors. Mayor David Wynne was the first mayor to be elected by the citizens.

Since the merger became effective on January 1, 1963, ten members of council have served as mayor of the City of Chesapeake; they are as follows:

Colon L. Hall	1963
Howard R. McPherson	1963
Guerdon A. Treakle	1965
William S. Overton	1970
Marian P. Whitehurst	1972
Sidney M. Oman	1980
J. Bennie Jennings	1984
Sidney M. Oman	1986
David I. Wynne	1988
William E. Ward	1990
William E. Ward	1992 to present

The grand opening of the new multi-million–dollar jail addition (correctional center) was held on Thursday May 29, 1997. According to Colonel Claude Stafford, undersheriff, who served as master of ceremonies, money for the facility

Members of the c. 1974 sheriff's color guard are, from left to right, Lieutenant Stafford, Lieutenant Caddle, Deputy Chebetar, Deputy Richardson, and Corporal Brickhouse.

This long building, which was constructed in phases, is the headquarters for Chesapeake's police and fire departments.

was acquired through the wheeling and dealing of Sheriff John Newhart, and the cost would not fall on the backs of the local taxpayers.

In 1998, construction of a new multi-story court building was begun across the street from the correctional center. It was occupied in September 1999.

CHESAPEAKE FIRE

That part of public safety that can be relied upon in case of fire is furnished by the Chesapeake Fire Department, whose roots go back to the many small volunteer units that existed in the villages and towns of Norfolk County and the City of South Norfolk. The ring of a fire bell or crude siren mounted on top of an old tin garage usually called the volunteers to action.

It was in 1892 that the village of South Norfolk first organized a volunteer fire department, with Captain George Funk as its chief. The equipment acquired by the department included an old hand-drawn reel and a few hundred feet of hose, both of which were stored in a dilapidated building located behind J.T. Lane's Drug Store on Liberty Street.

The department soon became inactive but a reorganization took place in 1909, and Captain Funk was again elected chief of the South Norfolk Volunteer Fire Department. In 1911, a horse-drawn hose reel was acquired from the Berkley Fire Department. Berkley had originally received it from Jamestown.

When the fire signal sounded, the reel and wagon was pulled by any horse in the community that was available. In 1915, Ira Johnson of the Greenleaf Johnson Lumber Company donated a mule for use by the department. As soon as possible, the mule was traded for a horse. Unfortunately, the horse ate itself out of a job and had to be sold to pay the feed bill. After that, D.W. Raper and Son Lumber Company donated the services of their horse to pull the equipment to and from the fires.

S. Herman Dennis Sr. became the second fire chief, and under his leadership, the department completely updated its equipment. A 500-gallon-per-minute American LaFrance was purchased, and a Ford truck chassis was converted to a hose wagon. This new equipment was paid for within two years. Around 1926, a new 1,000-gallon-per-minute American LaFrance pumper was purchased. Donations from the citizens and businesses of South Norfolk paid all but $6,000 of the debt. When Chief Dennis died in 1928, the equipment was conveyed to the City, and they paid the remaining amount.

In the early 1930s, a city hall was built on Liberty Street and the fire headquarters was moved to the first floor. W.F. Morgan was chief at that time and

South Norfolk's third fire station could be found on the first floor of the building to the right in this photograph. The two-story building also served as city hall at the time. The dual-purpose structure was built on Liberty Street sometime around 1930. The double house next door to the fire station was probably constructed in the early 1900s.

held the position until 1934, when he was succeeded by D.R. Gregory. Gregory stayed for one year and then left the department. L.H. Newberry was elected chief in 1935, and Forest G. Williams filled the new position of deputy chief.

By 1937, the fire department was operating the first ambulance in the city. Members of the department went door to door and held fund-raising events to pay for the unit. This new service was available free of charge, 24 hours a day, to all residents of South Norfolk, Portlock, and surrounding areas.

In late 1937, S. Herman Dennis Jr. followed L.H. Newberry as fire chief. At that time, the South Norfolk Fire Department was the best-equipped volunteer unit in the state of Virginia. There were 30 members, and they were paid by the hour while fighting fires. There was an average of 10 calls per month.

One evening in 1938, tragedy struck the department. The 1,000-gallon pumper was totaled when it collided with a Norfolk and Southern Jitney bus at the corner of Bainbridge Boulevard and Park Avenue. John W. Jernigan was killed and three other firemen were seriously injured. A new pumper was ordered from American LaFrance, and the wrecked one was stored in the old building, which had been Gregory's Blacksmith Shop at 700 Liberty Street.

In 1941, a new Cadillac ambulance was purchased at a cost of $4,000. This purchase was financed, as the other ambulance had been, by donations from the citizens, businesses, and local industrial plants.

A 750-gallons-per-minute LaFrance Quad was purchased in 1944 at a cost of $14,000. When the piece of equipment arrived, it was discovered that it was too large for the streets of South Norfolk. The City was able to recoup most of its investment by selling it to the City of Norfolk for $10,000. The Quad was placed in service at the Ocean View Fire Station.

When the City of South Norfolk changed to the city manager form of government in 1947, the fire department was again reorganized. At that time, R.D. Wallace was elected fire chief, and T.J. VanVleek, J.W. Dunning, and D.S. Ford became assistant chiefs. A fire prevention bureau was established with Ovie Yensen as chief of the bureau. This was the first fire prevention bureau established in the South Norfolk–Norfolk County region. When the City of Chesapeake was formed, T.J. VanVleek became its first fire marshall. In 1949, Forest Williams replaced Wallace as fire chief. It was also in 1949 that legal proceedings began for the annexation of the town of Portlock.

When South Norfolk annexed Portlock on January 1, 1951, the City of South Norfolk hired its first full-time employees to serve on the fire department. W.H. "Wink" Evans and John Ben Gibson Sr. were appointed deputy chiefs; Maxie L. Chappell, Vernon Eure, Stanley VanVleek, Peter Hollowell, Tom Sawyer, and George Gwynn were hired to operate the equipment. A short time later, Ovie Yensen was assigned the full-time position of fire inspector. Forest G. Williams, a volunteer, remained fire chief. The position of volunteer fire chief carried with it a salary of $100 per year.

Chief Williams died in 1953 and T.J. VanVleek was appointed to fill the vacancy. When Chief VanVleek resigned in 1954, John Ben Gibson Sr. became the first

This building in the Greenbrier area housed both the fire station and the fifth police precinct until recently. The police have since relocated to Research Drive.

full-time fire chief. A second battalion chief position was created in 1958, and Robert G. Bagley, who in later years would become the second fire chief of the City of Chesapeake, was appointed to fill the new opening.

In 1963, John Ben Gibson Sr. became the first fire chief of Chesapeake. Chief Gibson was one of a group of concerned citizens of Portlock that met in K.C. Karnegay's garage in November 1923 to address the issue of fire protection for the Village of Portlock. During this meeting, the Portlock Volunteer Fire Department was organized. The group elected A. Gallop as fire chief and W.S. O'Neal as president of the organization.

Their first equipment was an old hand reel and 200 feet of hose, which was donated by Norfolk County Supervisor Charlie Old. A large bell was mounted on the roof of the garage and was used to alert the volunteers when a fire call came in. The Gibson garage donated the department's first firetruck in 1925. The truck was a 1924 Model-T Ford and was used to tow the hand reel to the fire scene. Sheriff Wendel of Norfolk County gave the department a Buick automobile in 1926. Members converted the car into a truck and equipped it with additional hose, back tanks, and fire extinguishers.

In 1928, the school board granted the small fire department permission to construct a new station on the corner of school property located at Bainbridge Boulevard and Freeman Avenue. Sufficient funds were obtained to purchase building materials, and the members constructed the new fire station. The bell was replaced with a siren. In 1930, through the efforts of County Supervisor Wood, a Chevrolet firetruck was obtained. Because of its size, the station had to be enlarged and a new bay was added at this time.

Chief Gallop died in 1932 and E.H.Cuthrell was appointed to the position. C. Glemming was elected president, and after serving one year, he was succeeded by J.H. McCloud, who also served one year. In 1934, Cuthrell was reappointed as chief and began to receive a small salary for maintenance of the equipment. A.L. Capps was appointed to the position of assistant chief.

John Ben Gibson Sr. became the new chief in 1935 and held the position for many years. During his tenure, the department continued to progress and grow. Raincoats, boots, and other gear were purchased with funds received from Norfolk County.

The first ambulance, a 1930 Packard, was donated by Oscar F. Smith of Smith Douglas Fertilizer Corporation in 1938. The department began to solicit funds to buy a 1938 Cadillac to replace the Packard. The drive was successful, and the Cadillac was put into service in 1941.

In 1942, a 1941 GMC truck with a front-mounted pump was obtained for use as a second-run piece, and by 1943, the County had replaced the original first-run piece with a new 750-gallon Peter Pirsch pumper. Again, the station was too small

This fire at Crestwood was purposely set in order to train rookie members of the fire department. Pictured, from left to right, are the fire instructors: (front row) Brad Hennis and Barry Bailey; (back row) Steve Gurganus, Wayne Turner, Jimmy Smith, Pat McCarthy, and John Rudis.

for this new piece of equipment, and plans were made to build a larger one. The new station would have four bays, a workshop, an office, a meeting hall, and bedrooms. Norfolk County Supervisor Wilson Paxson secured the funds for the building. It was completed and dedicated in 1944.

Following the opening of the new station, the chief and assistant chief became full-time salaried employees. Two full-time firemen were also hired. The Portlock Fire Department served the areas of what is now Indian River, Greenbrier, Great Bridge, and everything south to the North Carolina line.

The development of the Cradock community began with the onset of World War I when housing was needed for additional government employees and military personnel. Cradock is not in the city of Chesapeake, but it was in earlier years a part of Norfolk County. It is now in the city of Portsmouth off George Washington Highway near the Norfolk Navy yard, which is itself also in Portsmouth, not Norfolk.

At the start of the war the area still contained Civil War gun mounts that had to be removed and trenches that needed to be filled before the new housing could be built. Its development was similar to those of small communities in New England, where fire and police protection was of primary importance. By 1919, Cradock was considered a city.

Its first fire station was a two-story building on Afton Parkway, which was equipped with a 750-gallon American LaFrance pumper that was furnished by the federal government. Two paid firefighters, a few volunteers, and several men furnished by the Marine Corps provided Cradock with ample fire protection.

By 1921, the community of Cradock was experiencing financial difficulties and asked Norfolk County to take it over. In 1922, it became part of Norfolk County. By late 1923, the Cradock Fire Department became the Cradock Volunteer Fire Department. The area began to grow, and the volunteers needed additional equipment. The Great Depression descended upon the area, and their plans had to be changed. Money was collected for a truck chassis, and using a chemical wagon obtained from Portsmouth, they built a motorized chemical wagon.

In 1935, the volunteer department became incorporated. The State Charter listed the following: L. Pederson (president); C.T. Smith (secretary); and V.E. Savvan, Jack Sherman, G.R. Hanrahan, F.H. Osborne, and Roger I.Keay (officers). In 1936, the department began offering first-aid medical services, and in 1939, it was able to acquire a second-hand ambulance. Funds were collected and a new ambulance was purchased in 1941.

During World War II, Cradock again received a heavy influx of military personnel and government employees, just as it had during World War I. The need for better fire protection was realized, and in 1944, a large, new brick station was built near the site of the original firehouse. By 1942 and 1943, the Ladies Auxiliary Ambulance Corp had been organized to help provide medical services; Ms. Elizabeth Hoffler had been appointed captain.

In 1947, Cradock's paid department consisted of four men: Donald S. Keay, Winifred Whitehurst, Arnold C. Barrow, and Melvin L. Atkins. Chief Keay later served Chesapeake as a battalion chief. Assistant Chief Whitehurst served Chesapeake as a fire captain. Atkins also served as a battalion chief for Chesapeake.

In 1958, plans were underway by the City of Portsmouth to annex a large area of Norfolk County, which would include Cradock. The Cradock Volunteer Fire Department soon became the Brentwood Volunteer Fire Department, and as mentioned, several of the members would begin serving the new City of Chesapeake in 1963.

Other county fire departments included Western Branch, which became operational on October 10, 1943, with F.B. Randlett as chief and H.O. Cupp as assistant chief. Fentress Fire Department began in 1946 with two paid employees, Hubert Swain and Clarence Curling. Both came from the Tanners Creek Department, which had been formed in 1942.

The new Great Bridge fire station opened in February 1948. It had been built by the combined efforts of the U.S. Army Corp of Engineers and Norfolk County. The Corp of Engineers furnished the land valued at $35,000 and the County invested approximately $10,000 in materials and labor. When the station opened, Clarence Curling was moved from Fentress to serve as chief and W.R. "Billy Ray" Powers was hired to serve as assistant chief.

Auxiliary Officer Bill Hodge, who was then an active-duty Navy diving corpsman, trained the Chesapeake Police Department's first dive team in 1973. This group appears to be practicing its rescue techniques.

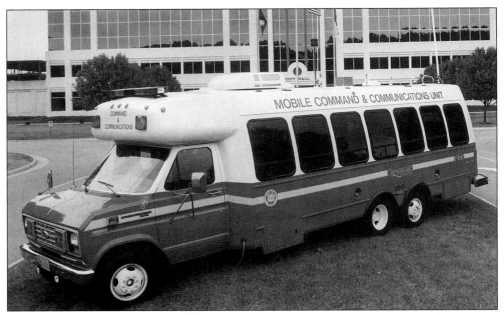

The Mobile Command and Communication Unit serves as a command center when normal power is lost for any reason, including during hurricanes.

After Portlock was annexed by the City of South Norfolk, the board of supervisors of Norfolk County made plans to build a fire station in the Washington District. The first chief was W.L. "Pete" Hollowell, who came from the Portlock station.

February 1957 was the beginning of the Deep Creek Fire Department and Rescue Squad. The citizens raised $800 to pay for the first ambulance, which in the beginning was green in color and was later painted white. In 1958, the final payment was made on the ambulance, and the department bought an aluminum boat to be used in water rescue. A local gas station was used as the department headquarters. The fire department was also organized during this period. An earlier attempt had been made in 1948, but was unsuccessful. E. Trigg Harrison, president of the local Ruritan Club, and other members of his committee were responsible for organizing and equipping the department in 1958. Harrison later became the first postmaster of the City of Chesapeake.

The Sunray Volunteer Fire Department, which was organized in December 1959, had no home but assisted other stations. Their first president was Paul Zydron Jr. It was not until the Chesapeake Fire Department opened station No.10 at Bowers Hill that the members from Sunray had a station to go to. In 1959, the St. Brides area was still without fire protection, and the nearest station was Great Bridge, which was a considerable distance away. Organization of the St. Brides Fire Department was a joint effort between the Pleasant Grove and Butts Road Districts of Norfolk County. L.A. Deford and Marvin Lee operated the new

This engine from the Chesapeake Fire Department is returning to station number 5 on Hanbury Road after answering a call.

department. In later years, Deford and Marvin Lee both retired from the Chesapeake Fire Department.

Since the City of Chesapeake was formed in 1963, it has had four men to serve as fire chief. The first was John Ben Gibson Sr., who was followed on January 1, 1970, by Robert G. Bagley. Bagley retired on July 1, 1986, and was replaced by Michael L. Bolac from the Alexandria Fire Department. After Bolac resigned, a nationwide search for a new chief revealed that the best qualified was already serving the city as assistant chief. R. Stephen Best, who began his career as a volunteer with the Deep Creek Department and became a paid firefighter in December 1974, received the job as Chesapeake fire chief.

In 2001, the Chesapeake Fire Department Employee Recognition Awards Ceremony was held on May 3. Firefighter/paramedic Jeffery L. Brennaman received Medic of the Year (2000), and firefighter/specialist John R. Rudis was awarded the trophy for Firefighter of the Year (2000).

The City of Chesapeake has grown by leaps and bounds since January 1, 1963. The beginning population was 75,000. In the year 2002 it is approximately 205,000 and still growing. Construction continues at a rapid rate with many new homes and apartments rising up throughout the city. Construction of a new five-lane bridge on Battlefield Boulevard has already begun and there are plans for a visitor's center near the new bridge   that will feature the stories of the Battle of Great Bridge and the Chesapeake and Albemarle Canals. All this helps Chesapeake's economy grow stronger.

155

The city seal was adopted on January 2, 1963, and is representative of both entities involved in the union. There are two figures shaking hands. The man on the left representing the rural population of Norfolk County with a background of fields, trees, and a home. The plow represents the agricultural aspect. The man on the right symbolizes the industrial community of South Norfolk with a factory in the background. The rising sun is symbolic of a bright future for the new city. The motto, "One Increasing Purpose," is taken from "Locksley Hall" by the poet Alfred Lord Tennyson.

In front of the public safety building stand two monuments, one dedicated to police officers who were killed in the line of duty and the other to fire fighters who lost their lives serving others. The police officers whose names appear on the memorial are Jasper C. Miller, Talbot D. Barrow, Berchman White, Ralph Steed, Ray P. Gallimore, and John H. Cherry. The fire fighters whose names appear on the memorial are A.L. Johnson, Capt. Sherman W. Goddin Sr., Jerrold W. Branch, John R. Hudgins Jr., and Frank E. Young.

BIBLIOGRAPHY

Chandler, Julian Alvin Carroll, Ed. *The South in the Building of the Nation, Volume I: History of the States*. Richmond, VA: The Southern Historical Publication Society, 1909.

Dickinson, Sue V. *The First Sixty Years*. Bristol, UK: Imperial Tobacco Company of Great Britain and Ireland, 1962.

Harper, Raymond L. History of South Norfolk: 1661–1963. Chesapeake, VA: Self-published, 1996.

———. *Images of America: South Norfolk*. Charleston, SC: Arcadia Publishing, 1999.

———. *Images of America: Norfolk County*. Charleston, SC: Arcadia Publishing, 2000.

Porter, John W.H. History of Norfolk County: 1861-1865. Portsmouth, VA: W.A. Fiske, 1892.

Tyler, Lyon Gardner, Ed. *Encyclopedia of Virginia Biography. Volumes IV and V*. N.p.: Lewis Historical Publishing Co., 1915.

Whichard, Rogers Dey. *The History of Lower Tidewater Virginia, Volumes I and II*. N.p.: Lewis Historical Publishing Co., 1959.

Newspapers

TIPS Weekly, Berkley Edition. Feb. 26, 1898.

Chesapeake Clipper. May 1983, 1995–1998.

Chesapeake Post. April 21, 1966; 1995–1998.

The Norfolk Landmark. Sept. 16, 1878; 1903–1904; May 19, 1912.

The Norfolk Ledger-Dispatch. Aug. 9, 1919.

The Norfolk Virginian-Pilot. Dec. 17, 1911; April 4, 1926; Sept.12, 1937; June 19, 1938; Dec. 23, 1961; April 15, 2001.

The Virginian-Pilot and *The Ledger-Star*. June 26, 1994.

Virginia-Carolina News. Dec. 29, 1960; Jan. 11, 1962; Feb. 1, 1962.

Periodicals, Minutes, and Miscellany

American Heritage. March 1990. Forbes, Inc.

Chesapeake's Museum and Information Center. Minutes of September 1990–December 2000.

Code of South Norfolk, Virginia. 1946 and 1952.

Colonna Papers. Volume I, July 1988; Volume II, May 1996. Chesapeake's Museum, VA.

Fifteenth Anniversary Program. South Norfolk Athletic Association, April 15, 1939.

Norfolk County, its History and Development—The Leading County of Virginia. Author and publisher unknown.

Renewal, Vol. 3, No. 1. Berent, Irwin M. "A History of Tidewater Jewry." Norfolk, VA: United Jewish Federation of Tidewater, 1986.

St. Matthew's Catholic Church—The Fiftieth Anniversary. The Rudis family.

The Berkley Lineage—A History of the First Berkley Family of Norfolk, VA. Waverly Berkley III.

Virginia Cavalcade. The quarterly illustrated magazine of Virginia history and culture. The Library of Virginia, 1999.

Vital Signs, Chesapeake Health. Chesapeake General Hospital, December 2000.

INDEX